# 10 STRATEGIES FOR MAKING YOUR AGE AN ADVANTAGE IN YOUR CAREER

# over-40 JOB SEARCH GUIDE

GAIL GEARY, JD

# Over-40 Job Search Guide

© 2005 by Gail Geary

Published by JIST Works, an imprint of JIST Publishing, Inc.
8902 Otis Avenue
Indianapolis, IN 46216-1033
Phone: 1-800-648-JIST          Fax: 1-800-JIST-FAX          E-mail: info@jist.com

Visit our Web site at **www.jist.com** for information on JIST, free job search tips, book chapters, and ordering instructions for our many products! For free information on 14,000 job titles, visit **www.careeroink.com**.

> Quantity discounts are available for JIST books.
> Please call our Sales Department at 1-800-648-5478 for a free catalog and more information.

Acquisitions Editor: Lori Cates Hand
Development Editor: Barb Terry
Interior and Cover Designer: designLab, Seattle
Page Layout: Nick Anderson
Proofreader: Linda Seifert
Indexer: Tina Trettin

Printed in Canada
08 07 06 05      9 8 7 6 5 4 3 2

Library of Congress Cataloging-in-Publication Data

Geary, Gail, 1943-
Over-40 job search guide : 10 strategies for making your age an advantage in your career / Gail Geary.
      p. cm.
Includes index.
ISBN 1-59357-090-2
1. Job hunting. 2. Middle aged persons--Employment. I. Title: Over-forty job search guide. II. Title.
HF5382.7.G43 2005
650.14'084'4--dc22

                              2004018201

ISBN 1-59357-090-2

# About This Book

Blatant (and subtle) age discrimination exists in today's highly competitive job market. As a mature career seeker, you have two choices: You can unconsciously sabotage yourself, reinforcing negative age-related stereotypes. *Or* you can be your own best career search friend, "wowing" a future employer with your impressive, updated ageless resume; your stylish and energetic self-presentation; and your savvy interview skills. Fortunately, you don't have to do it on your own.

Gail Geary gives you the insider's slant on what works and what doesn't based on 12 years of experience presenting workshops and coaching to more than 1,200 clients in the process of individual career transition and as part of major companies experiencing downsizing in industry sectors including manufacturing, telecommunications, technology, retail, and financial services.

With Gail's expert advice, you can reenergize your career, revise your vision, or totally reinvent yourself—in the corporate world or in an entrepreneurial venture. This book provides truthful answers to your career search questions through case studies, clear examples, and interactive exercises.

*Over-40 Job Search Guide* is the premier job search guide for mature workers, devoted exclusively to providing effective solutions for your career search needs.

# CONTENTS

# INTRODUCTION

Y ou hold in your hands the only career transition guide to exclusively provide workable solutions for the re-employment issues facing the over-40 worker. How do you know that you can rely on this guide to meet your needs? Read on!

## How Can This Book Help You?

The United States has faced an increase in unemployed older workers. In recent years, employee downsizing has resulted in the loss of 1.6 million jobs, with Americans in the over-40 age group suffering the heaviest casualties. Why is this so?

During economic downturn, employers achieve immediate improvement in their bottom line when they lay you off–their highest-paid employee, the one who usually happens to be their most reliable and most experienced worker. You, the employee who has given the most and performed the best, are suddenly without work.

Finding yourself out of work, you then face another discouraging hurdle: discrimination in hiring. Although you might not be able to present a defensible Equal Employment Opportunity lawsuit, you nevertheless face employers who harbor negative and stereotypical opinions about older workers.

You will also find your career dreams ambushed by well-meaning family and friends with mistaken impressions about careers that are "age appropriate." And frequently you will also have to address your own negative self-talk. The guidance in this book will help you combat these unacknowledged enemies.

## What's Inside This Book?

Each chapter of *Over-40 Job Search Guide* thoroughly and humorously prepares you to successfully manage your own career search:

- Chapter 1, "Play It Again on Your Own Terms," gives you the information you need to determine whether it's time to make a career change and explore related and different career options.

- Chapter 2, "Play to Your Strengths," helps you identify and promote the distinct age advantages that you bring to the career marketplace.

- Chapter 3, "Uncover What's Hot and What's Not," reveals the positions and industries that are financially healthy, hiring, and age-diverse.

- Chapter 4, "Acquire Inexpensive Skill and Credential Updates," shares how to jump-start a new career or revive a current or past career by updating your skills and credentials.

- Chapter 5, "Create a *Wow!* Ageless Resume," shows you how to design a resume that emphasizes your strengths and experience and de-emphasizes your age.

- Chapter 6, "Find Age-Diverse Job Opportunities," gives you cutting-edge information to conduct strategic searches off- and online.

- Chapter 7, "Achieve Memorable First Impressions," shows you how to avoid common interview and networking mistakes and how to leave a lasting positive impression.

- Chapter 8, "Ace Tough Interview Questions," gives you the best practical advice for avoiding discrimination and negotiating your best offer.

- Chapter 9, "Explore the Road Less Traveled," shows that you're never too old to uncover entrepreneurial ventures and self-employment opportunities.

- Chapter 10, "Too Young to Quit Working," opens the doors to new careers and volunteer activities for post-retirement years.

## Take Charge of Your Own Career

Being over 40 does not have to mean terminal unemployment or chronic underemployment. You have the edge over younger and less experienced workers. It's only a matter of promoting your strengths and watching out for those "age ambushes." And, indications are that within the next few years, the demand for people of your age in the workplace will be increasing because the next generation is smaller.

Stop listening to the naysayers. Relax, get involved with this book, and get your career on track!

## Who Is Gail Geary?

*Over-40 Job Search Guide: Ten Strategies for Making Your Age an Advantage in Your Career* is the work of one of the most respected experts in career transition today. For the last 12 years, Gail has consciously chosen an entrepreneurial practice composed of business and career consulting. She regularly conducts continuing-education seminars and has been on the adjunct faculty for the American Management Association and three Atlanta-area universities. On a daily basis, Gail presents workshops, coaches career-transition clients, conducts mock interviewing sessions, and presents negotiation and self-marketing labs for Right Management Consultants. For the last three years, she has conducted a special workshop, "How to Use Age as an Advantage in Your Career Search." As if that weren't enough, Gail is a member of the Georgia and Atlanta Bar Associations and uses her expertise to keep abreast of legal issues regarding careers, particularly those involving age discrimination.

Gail knows firsthand what she's teaching others. She successfully transitioned from a career as an English, speech, and drama teacher to the position of Corporate Counsel for the Aon Group, an international commercial insurance and human resources consulting firm. She then transitioned into its sales department, becoming the top salesperson internationally out of 17,000 employees and Senior Vice President of Sales and Marketing. Her personal experiences in career transition, downsizing, reorganization, mergers, and acquisitions give Gail a practical, as well as academic, perspective.

# For More Personal Help with Your Career

I would love to hear from you. I can support you in all these aspects of your career search, in person and by telephone or e-mail:

- Career assessment
- Resume and cover letter development
- Strategic mailing list preparation
- Interview practice
- Negotiation practice
- Strategic career advancement
- Executive image enhancement
- Entrepreneurial/self-employment venture development
- Business plan assistance

I am also available as a dynamic presenter to your organization on career-related topics. Contact me at

**Gail Geary**
Atlanta Career Transition
gail@atlantacareertranstion.com
www.atlantacareertransiton.com
1-888-670-4157 or 770-804-8449

# CHAPTER 1

## Play It Again on Your Own Terms
### Explore Your Career Options and Develop Your Ideal Career

*"Life is like playing a violin in public and learning the instrument as one goes on."*

*—Samuel Butler*

The good news is this: You do have the time to learn and play a new musical score, and to experience the joy of career renewal or the birth of an entirely new career. Career transition is a precious gift, a time for you to pause and truly reflect, maybe for the first time, on what you want to do in the second and third stages of your life.

If you are consciously choosing a career change, you may find the career transition experience stimulating and enjoyable. On the other hand, if you have been a part of a corporate reorganization, downsizing, or unexpected lifestyle change, you may be asking yourself the "why me, and why now?" questions.

For whatever reasons you find yourself in the job search or career-development mode, you can revel in the fact that you are over 40. Why? Because you have a competitive edge over a younger worker. Your past work and volunteer experiences provide you with many more career options than you had as a young adult fresh out of school. And your wisdom allows you to explore and exploit your options in choosing your ideal next career.

## What Is Your Ideal Career?

Your ideal career expresses your desires in relationship to the current and future job marketplace. It's about satisfying your expectations in these five essential areas:

- Interests
- Abilities
- Career marketability
- Earnings
- Values and lifestyle

The following sections show just how these areas relate to those of us who are over 40.

*The essential ingredients of your ideal career.*

## Interests

Your career choice should mirror your interests. To identify your interests, I recommend that you use a combination of formal and informal assessments and match them to actual career positions.

## Informal Assessments

These are a few of the informal ways to discover your interests. Make a note of what you discover.

- Look at your yearly calendar and take an inventory of how you have spent your leisure time in the last three months. What interests are reflected?

- Look at your on- or offline checkbook and credit-card statements for clues on how you have spent your discretionary income in the last three months. What interests did you support?

- Check the Sunday career section of your local paper and circle all the careers that interest you. Did you find anything that excited you?

Aerial, one of my clients, age 61, discovered a position of great interest in the newspaper, a Director of Outdoor Wilderness Activities for a coed camp in the mountains. His combination of volunteer and paid experience qualified him for this position, and he is thrilled about the challenge. When I asked him whether this interest was reflected in his checkbook and credit-card statements, he answered in the affirmative. He is in the process of taking a Wilderness First Responder Course to round out his credentials.

## Formal Assessments

The best way to formally match your interests to actual career positions is to take an interest inventory such as the *Transition-to-Work Inventory* or the *Leisure/Work Search Inventory* by Dr. John Liptak (both available from JIST Publishing; www.jist.com) or the *Self-Directed Search* by John Holland (available at www.self-directed-search.com). These inventories match your interests to actual career positions. Other excellent career-preference inventories include the Myers-Briggs Type Indicator and the Strong Interest Inventory that can be purchased from and interpreted by an individual career counselor or through multiple online career sources.

David, one of my career clients, took the *Transition-to-Work Inventory* and discovered that his interests fell into three occupational clusters/interest groups: arts, entertainment, and media; plants and animals; and sales and marketing. As many people have discovered, David's past careers did match his interests. He had been a broadcast journalist and a furniture salesman, careers that fit in the media and sales clusters. David admitted that he would love to be a cat veterinarian or forest ranger, but at 59, felt that a career as a mortgage loan officer would take less time to develop while still expressing his interest in sales and marketing. And, he had eight cats and two young kids at home, anyway.

## Ability

After you decide that you are interested in a career, determine whether you need to update or obtain new skills or credentials to make yourself a prime fit for the position. In some cases, just changing the emphasis of your resume to highlight transferable experience and using a functional resume will be sufficient, because you already have the ability to do the job based on past experience. In Chapter 5, I'll cover how to design a resume to emphasize your strengths and turn your past experience into a new career.

David chose to pursue a career as a mortgage loan officer because of his interest in sales and marketing and because he was able to obtain credentials in a short time at a reasonable cost. His certification cost $500 and took a week to obtain. You will enjoy reading about many inexpensive skill and credential updates in Chapter 4.

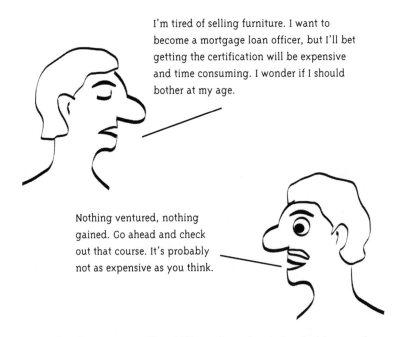

I'm tired of selling furniture. I want to become a mortgage loan officer, but I'll bet getting the certification will be expensive and time consuming. I wonder if I should bother at my age.

Nothing ventured, nothing gained. Go ahead and check out that course. It's probably not as expensive as you think.

*Negative Stereotype: The skills and credentials of older workers are not up-to-date.*

## Marketability

After determining that you have an interest in a career position and that you are able to affordably update your skills and credentials in a reasonable time frame, you must determine whether your career choice is marketable in today's economy and is age diverse. We look more closely at viable career options in Chapter 3.

Robert, 48, a vice president of sales in technology, spent a year hitting career-search dead ends. During his search, the telecommunications industry was in a mass downsizing mode, with few new hires. Having majored in biology in college, Robert wisely revitalized his past interest in the subject and became a high school biology teacher and baseball coach. He loves the challenge of his job, but does miss his six-digit earnings. Robert's wife, Judy, has returned to work to supplement the family income. They maintain a flexible attitude toward the future.

Like Robert, you may find yourself in the position of accepting a job that is not your first choice. Not to worry. Yours is not a life-or-death choice. The market will invariably turn, and new doors will open for you. If you accept that less-than-perfect job for now, you will be relieved, knowing that you did not seriously deplete your retirement savings or put your family in financial peril.

## Earnings

As you investigate your career options, take the time to determine the earnings potential of the position that interests you. Will it support your lifestyle? Will you need to supplement it? How does your family feel about your choice? You can easily check out the salary range for a position of interest in the city where you will be working at www.salary.com or www.monster.com.

Sophia was interested in and fascinated by the position of mediator; but, through a salary survey and two information interviews, she learned that she would be paid only $25 to $50 for inconsistent court-appointed mediations. Because of immediate earning needs, she decided to consider mediation as a volunteer option for her leisure time and her retirement years.

## Values and Lifestyle

Does your career choice match your values (or principles) and lifestyle preferences, such as your need for solitude or socialization, or your desire for a short commute or international travel? When you are involved in or considering a career move, you have an excellent opportunity to consider more than salaries. You can also focus on challenge, relationships, values, and the lifestyle you want.

Steve is a former "big firm" consultant who traveled 75 percent of the time in his job. He recently shared with me that he is gladly taking a small decrease in salary for a challenging, local work environment and more time with his family. He is wise to recognize that earnings are only one part of the ideal job equation. Values and lifestyle are equally important.

Considering these five essential career elements—interests, abilities, career marketability, earnings, and values and lifestyle—before you move forward will prevent you from wasting time or getting stuck in a career you hate. Use the following worksheet to make a few notes about what you know now and what you need to discover to determine your ideal career.

---

### What Are the Key Elements of My Ideal Career?

My interests


My abilities


My career marketability


My earnings requirements


My values and lifestyle

---

## Exploring New Games: Your Career Options

Why shouldn't you play the old game? What are the new games? In the popular book *Who Moved My Cheese?*, by Spencer Johnson and Kenneth Blanchard, two rats, Sniff and Scurry, lose their supply of cheese. For a long time, they keep returning to the same rat restaurant (have you eaten there too?) to find their cheese, but to no avail. Finally, they smarten up and realize that they must change directions to locate new sources of food. Fortunately, they are successful.

In my practice as a career counselor, I see candidates who, like Sniff and Scurry, continue to look for their cheese (careers) in the same places. In my experience, I have found that the most difficult career choice for a mature worker is to try to resurrect a career that is no longer viable in today's economy or is in an unreasonably youth-oriented industry.

It is possible to play the old game, to seek a similar position in your most recent industry, but this may not be the best choice if your industry no longer supplies your cheese. If the industry is not financially healthy, hiring, and age diverse, you may need to explore and exploit your other options. In Chapter 3 we'll explore specific careers that are financially healthy, hiring, and age diverse.

Statistically, mature workers generally take a month longer to locate a new job or career, not only because of age discrimination in the workplace, but also because they are choosing to explore different career options and reinventing themselves and their careers. You have five viable career options right now. You can choose to pursue

- A comparable position within your most recent industry
- A different position within your most recent industry
- A comparable position in a different industry
- An entirely new position in a different industry
- Concurrent careers, which means that you work in multiple careers on a part-time or contract basis

You can also take the entrepreneurial route of self-employment, which we will explore in Chapter 9.

How can you begin sifting through these options to find the right one for you? The next few sections share issues you will want to consider as you begin to make a decision.

## Staying in the Same Industry

The first commandment of career transition, and often the most difficult to follow, is to choose a career that is marketable. A marketable career is one that you can secure before your severance or career transition budget runs out and you tap deeply and dangerously into your retirement income. The most obvious choice is to search for a comparable position within the industry that you most recently worked, but your interests, your age, and the financial health of the industry may not make this a viable option.

### Choosing a Comparable Position in Your Most Recent Industry

Here are a few of the questions that you should ask yourself before pursuing a comparable position in the same industry:

- Is the position still interesting to me?
- Do I like the type of people working in the industry? The customers or clients? The products or services? The contribution the industry makes to society?
- Do I have a strong network of associates in the industry?
- Did I leave in good standing?
- Is the industry age diverse, and, if not, am I prepared to do what it takes to compete?
- Is the earning potential adequate for my future needs?
- Are my values and lifestyle preferences supported?
- Is the industry financially healthy and hiring?

Jean was vice president and general manager of a $50 million, upscale department store. After her 31st work anniversary and as part of a major corporate downsizing and reorganization, she was offered an attractive severance package and took it. When she came to our career-transition services, I heard from another consultant that she was pursuing a comparable position in the same industry, and I thought to myself, "Why does she still want to work in a retail environment, which is not notably age diverse and has been in a downsizing mode?" And, "Can she compete with a 35-year-old candidate?" This was before I met Jean in person. I interviewed Jean formally in a video mock-interviewing session and later at a networking event after she landed her dream job. I had some of my questions answered in the interview. The rest of my questions were answered in a private meeting with her.

Jean was extremely well prepared for the mock-interview session—from her positive physical first impression to her well-rehearsed interview answers. It was apparent in our interview that Jean was sincerely interested in continuing in retail management and that she still felt that this position and industry fully supported her earnings, values, and lifestyle preferences. In my opinion, she aced the interview.

After landing her dream job two months later, Jean shared with me the details of her transformation from a slightly overweight, matronly interview novice with no resume or formal interview skills to this highly marketable candidate. Before entering the career search, Jean had dropped 15 pounds, had endured a cosmetic facelift, and had taken advantage of all the job search classes and counseling offered by her former employer.

Jean recognized that she was swimming against the current by seeking a comparable position in a youth-dominated, frequently downsizing industry. She also knew, however, that retail management met her interests, ability, earnings potential, and values and lifestyle preferences. Her career marketability was an issue because of her age. But, as we learned, she was up to the challenge. Go, Jean!

If Jean had been tired of retail management, she could have revived an earlier career in retail sales. A third option would have been to pursue a management position in a different industry. Or, Jean might have taken a dramatic step and developed an entirely different career in a different industry. Let's take a look at how you can develop an entirely different career in the same industry.

## Developing a Different Position in Your Most Recent Industry

One of the advantages of being a 40-plus job seeker is that you may have multiple years of transferable experience that enable you to work in a different position in the same industry. You may have worked in a number of different positions prior to your last position, or you may have acquired the necessary skills and ability to work in a new position and just need to combine them and present them in a different way. Now you can take advantage of your experience!

These are the questions you need to ask yourself when considering a different career in your most recent industry:

- Is the industry still interesting to me?
- Do I like the type of people working in the industry? The customers or clients? The products or services? The contribution the industry makes to society?
- Do I have a strong network of associates in the industry?
- Is the industry financially healthy, hiring, and age diverse?
- Is the earning potential adequate for my future needs?
- Are my values and lifestyle preferences supported?
- Do I need additional skills or credentials to make the position change?

Here is how one of my career clients prepared herself for a different position in the same industry: Shara had 30-plus years of experience in the insurance industry. She began her professional career as an administrative assistant when she was 18 years old and over the years was promoted to a data coordinator and then to an account executive. For many years, Shara had dreamed of going into sales. She loved working with clients and had proven that she could support difficult and demanding accounts. Her decision to change positions was motivated by interest and earnings potential. She loved the idea of selling as well as servicing accounts, and a position in sales would dramatically increase her income.

Shara felt that she had the necessary sales ability based on her transferable experience from other positions, but one hurdle remained. She had no formal education or credentials for a sales position, and a future employer might discount her ability if it were based solely on past experience.

To cover her bases, Shara updated her credentials by attending a well-known sales course, *Strategic Selling* (see www.millerheiman.com), and passing with flying colors. Then she obtained her insurance agent's license by persuading a friend who owned an insurance agency to sponsor her.

Shara's next hurdle was to create a "*Wow!* ageless resume" in a functional format, allowing her to highlight her sales-related experiences from her administrative, data coordinator, and account executive positions. (You can learn more about writing resumes in Chapter 5.) To enhance her career potential, Shara was careful to emphasize the names of the key accounts she managed. Shara received a wonderful offer and a sign-on bonus and has never looked back.

Shara was in her mid-40s when she made the successful career change from account management to sales. She never earned a college degree, but consistently updated her skills and her appearance. She played to her strengths, which you will learn more about in Chapter 2.

## Transitioning to a Different Industry

If you're kicking a dead horse, it's time to choose a fresh mount! You've seen from the preceding two positive examples that wide ranges of career alternatives are available to you, but sometimes staying in the same industry may not be feasible in today's economy. The industries you are looking at may not be financially healthy, hiring, or age diverse. If you're kicking a dead horse, it's time for you to choose a fresh mount, which means choosing a totally new industry. You can tell it's time to change your career when

- Your severance pay or career-transition budget is about to or has run out.
- Your physical and mental energy is depleted.
- Your interviews are infrequent or nonexistent.
- You have received no job offers.
- Your significant other is sharing your problem with others.

You may think I'm kidding about that last point, but I'm not. While speaking at the American Business Women's Association's national conference on the topic of "Using Change to Reinvent Yourself and Your Business," I was surprised to learn that the number-one challenge facing the 400 women in my audience did not involve their own careers; it was getting their husbands back to work. In conversations and surveys during and after the conference, I learned that in the majority of cases, the 40-plus male spouse had been trying unsuccessfully to land the same job in the same industry. In most cases, the industry was unhealthy, or his competition was 20- and 30-year-olds. The husband continued unsuccessfully to pursue a position for which he was no longer marketable and became increasingly depressed the longer he was out of work. It was time for him to look at a different career option, but his ego kept getting in the way.

The following sections detail your options for when it's time to look at changing industries.

## Choosing a Similar Position in a Different Industry

As you reexamine your career interests, you may find that your position still interests you, but you no longer feel positive about working in the same industry. The industry may not be financially healthy, hiring, and age diverse, or you may no longer find that it supports other elements of your ideal career such as your earnings, lifestyle, and values.

These are the kinds of questions you need to ask yourself before pursuing a similar position in the same industry:

- Is this position still interesting to me?
- Why am I interested in the new industry?
- Do I have contacts in the new industry?
- Is the industry financially healthy, hiring, and age diverse?
- Will the earnings potential be adequate for my future needs?
- Are my values and lifestyle preferences supported?
- Will I need to obtain new skills or credentials to make this transition?

Let's discover why Diana decided to pursue a similar position in a new industry.

Diana married for the first time when she was in her early 40s and moved to Atlanta. She was a former executive recruiter, but was tired of recruiting and accepted a job in elementary education. After two years, she found that her teaching job was not meeting her earnings or lifestyle preferences. She felt that her pay was low, and she had several hours of homework a day. Teaching gave her little time to enjoy her husband and home, or to pursue her passion for tennis. Diana loved the position of teaching, but wanted to parlay her teaching experience and ability into another career with higher earnings potential and more freetime.

Diana designed a resume with a focus on adult education that highlighted achievements in her teaching and recruiting experience. While networking with a neighbor, she found an ideal adult teaching position in a career-transition firm, teaching adults job search skills. The firm provided on-the-job training, which built on her former teaching experience. She is on the adjunct staff, which means that she has many days off to enjoy her marriage and home, and to play a mean game of tennis. She does have homework, frequently editing multiple resumes after a workshop, but at least this home-work is not part of her daily routine. Diana has found a close-to-ideal job as measured by interests, ability, earnings, and values and lifestyle, as well as career marketability.

## Choosing a Different Career in a Different Industry

When you choose a different career in a different industry, you are really playing a brand new game. Whether you are displaced, dis-contented in your current career, or reentering the job market after a number of nonworking years, the process of reinventing yourself and your career can be confusing, but highly rewarding. Before tak-ing this leap, you should ask yourself the following questions:

- Am I deeply intrigued by a different position and industry and up to the double challenge of mastering a new position and a new industry?
- Can I obtain the necessary skills and credential updates in a reasonable time and within my budget?
- Does this career provide the necessary earnings potential?
- Is this career one that is age diverse and marketable in today's economy?
- Does this career have viability for the future?
- Will this career be a match for my values and lifestyle preferences?
- Am I making an emotional and a logical choice?

I have personal experience with multiple careers involving different positions in different industries. When I was 47 years old, I was senior vice president of sales and marketing for an international insurance brokerage. After 14 years, I had achieved the distinctions of first being an administrative assistant, their corporate attorney, then their top international sales professional, and finally senior vice president. I had a six-figure income, a posh office with an ori-ental carpet and oil paintings, a sizable annual bonus, and many friends at work and among my clients. So why would I fantasize about flying away on my carpet?

Because my company was consistently downsizing, reorganizing, and merging, I felt not only unstable, but also unchallenged. It seemed to me that I had hit the glass ceiling for a woman in my company. My friends and my family thought that I was nuts to think of leaving because we all had benefited from exotic trips and financial success. But I decided that my career satisfaction was worth the price, and I was ready for a change.

One morning at work, after a really short exploration into a career as an interior designer (one quarter of coursework), I saw an advertisement in the *Wall Street Journal* for CareerTrac seminar instructors. The ad gave a phone number to call and indicated that interested parties should send a video of an hour-long speaking presentation. Although I did not join CareerTrac, I did become an American Management Association instructor. I used my transferable legal, presentation, sales, and professional development skills from positions in law and corporate sales management to create a new career in professional development services. I started two businesses, Geary Communications and Atlanta Career Transition.

I have happily found in my 50s that counseling individual clients and conducting career-transition workshops is my passion. My career meets all my essential needs, including interests, ability, career marketability, and values and lifestyle. I do not make a comparable salary to the sales and marketing position I held, but being able to support my value and lifestyle preferences involving creative expression and time flexibility has made this career change worthwhile.

## Choosing Concurrent Positions in the Same or Different Industry

Many mature workers work in multiple positions, even in multiple industries, not only to increase their income, but also to enjoy the variety of experiences associated with different work. And flexible hours are a real benefit. The cost cuttings in the technology, manufacturing, and telecommunications industries actually benefit freelancers, who work in concurrent positions.

Matrix Resources and other staffing-solution firms are noticing an increasing demand for contract workers. Using a contingent workforce allows employers greater flexibility to control their costs. I have noticed a definite shift away from permanent work, and the Employment Policy Foundation, a data research organization, predicts that self-employment will increase to 10 percent of our workforce in the next few years.

To consider whether you are a candidate for working in concurrent positions, ask yourself these questions:

- Have I covered my bases in terms of health insurance?
- Am I self-disciplined and have I or can I put away savings for my own retirement?
- Do I enjoy work variety, or would I prefer a more structured environment?
- Do these concurrent positions interest me?
- Does this flexible work meet my values and lifestyle preferences?
- Can I successfully multitask?

Laura, age 52, was formally trained as a dental assistant, but when she divorced and moved to Atlanta she felt bored and unchallenged. She unconsciously took the concurrent career route, becoming more career eclectic and open to freelance positions. In the past two years, she has freelanced as a bartender for exclusive parties at the Holiday Inn Crowne Plaza, has been a caregiver for my mother, has assisted in the installation of a Colonial Gas pipeline (by driving a forklift, believe it or not), has worked for the IRS at tax time, and has assisted in the creation of my Web site. She is not afraid to use her current skills and talents and develop new ones.

You can make an exceptionally good income by working concurrent jobs, but you may have to work long hours.

---

### What Game Do You Want to Play?

1. Do you plan to seek a similar job in your most recent industry or a different job in the same or different industry? Do you need more time and information to make this decision?

   _____

2. Does your career choice meet your criteria in terms of interest, ability, earnings, career marketability, values, and lifestyle preferences? What additional research do you need to make to determine this?

   _____

   _____

3. What points in this chapter are significant to you personally?

   _____

   _____

# CHAPTER 2

## Play to Your Strengths
### Identify and Promote Your Age Advantages

*"To use fear as the friend it is, we must retrain and reprogram ourselves...we must persistently and convincingly tell ourselves that the fear is here...with its gift of energy and heightened awareness...so we can do our best and learn the most in the new situation."*

*—Peter McWilliams, Life 101*

On a good day, you truly believe that you have the competitive edge over younger workers because of your work and volunteer experience and life wisdom. But then the nagging voice of self-doubt rears its ugly head.

Carolyn, an attractive woman in her 50s, approached me in the hall on a workshop break. "I'm worried that my age is going to present a problem in finding employment. I'm worried that companies might discriminate against me because of my age," she said. Carolyn vocalized a concern shared by many mature workers. Hiring managers and companies do sometimes blatantly and subtly discriminate against older workers, based on negative stereotypes such as overqualification and cultural incompatibility (not able to fit in with a youth culture).

It's wise to open your eyes and take a look at your fears. Use your heightened awareness of the possibilities of age discrimination to give you increased energy for a proactive job search, which involves promoting the age-related advantages that you have over a younger worker. This chapter will help you identify your advantages and overcome the stereotypes you might face.

## Identifying Your Age-Related Advantages

This chapter is different from the others in that I'm going to ask you to get to work right from the beginning. I'd like for you to answer a question as honestly and thoughtfully as you can. Here goes.

What are the advantages that you as a mature worker bring to the table?

Over the last several years, I have asked this question to several hundred over-40 people in the career-transition process. Another way to come up with an answer to my question is to do this: Describe your professional strengths compared to those of a younger worker. Remember, the advantages and strengths that you select should represent benefits to a potential employer. The process of answering this question is a feel-good experience that can build your self-esteem, prepare you for writing your Wow! ageless resume, and help you ace tough interview questions.

To get you started, following is one of my age advantages or strengths. I share with you how I use it in my resume and in networking and interview situations.

| Advantage or Strength | Where Do I Use It? | How Do I State It? |
|---|---|---|
| Excellent, professional presentation skills | Resume, interviews, and presentation delivery | I mention that my high energy level, excellent delivery skills, and facilitation expertise ensure a positive learning experience for my clients. |

I attract new speaking and training opportunities by the words I use to describe myself in my resume, professional profile, and other advertising materials. I attract repeat speaking business and referral business through my delivery and facilitation expertise.

I have no doubt that you can find energetic presenters under 40 years old, but they are rarely able to deliver and facilitate at a professional level. I have cultivated this advantage or strength with years of practice and multiple audience experiences.

It's your turn. Take some time to complete the following worksheet. Now is not the time to be modest. Toot your own horn.

## What Are Your 10 Age Advantages or Strengths?

Use the spaces below to list your own advantages and strengths and how you will use them in your job campaign. Be specific.

| Advantage or Strength | Where Can I Use It? | How Will I State It? |
|---|---|---|
| 1. | | |
| 2. | | |
| 3. | | |
| 4. | | |
| 5. | | |
| 6. | | |
| 7. | | |
| 8. | | |
| 9. | | |
| 10. | | |

# Comparing Age-Related Advantages and Strengths

How do your advantages and strengths compare with those of other people in the over-40 age group? Following are some of the comments people in career transition make about their age-related strengths and how they plan to use these strengths in the career-transition process. They give you permission to borrow from their comments.

## Multigenerational Skills

Susan listed multigenerational skills as one of her advantages. Here is how she says she uses it:

- "In my resume, I say that I am an effective leader of multigenerational teams.

- "In answer to an interview question about my strengths or as a summary at the end of the interview, I say that I am skilled in building and effectively leading multigenerational teams and I provide a positive example.

- "Here is my proof. In the Memphis office of Air Express, I recently led a team consisting of one intern, one recent college graduate, four mature workers, and one part-time retiree. I was commended by senior management for team creativity and for coming in below budget on our project."

Recognizing your strengths is one thing. Being able to put them on paper and describe them in person as Susan did is the next important step. In Chapter 5 you'll discover how to design a resume to emphasize your strengths. In Chapter 7, you'll learn how to emphasize those strengths in networking and interviews.

## Broad Transferable Professional and Volunteer Experience

Paul, a tennis pro, became tired of the financial uncertainty of his entrepreneurial tennis business and decided to seek a position in sales with a sporting-goods manufacturer. One strength he chose to emphasize was his broad transferable professional and volunteer experience. He says:

- "In my resume, I wrote that I was qualified by 15 years of successful sales experience in the sporting-goods industry.

- "My proof was that I generated over $150,000 annually through the sale of tennis services, equipment, and clothing.

- "When an interviewer asked how my experience as a tennis pro translated into a sales career, I expanded on the experiences I included in my resume.

- "I also shared in my resume and interview my successful volunteer experience promoting charity tennis events."

Many times volunteer, nonprofit experience can translate into an added achievement or even a new career itself. One of my clients became the director of a resort based on his volunteer experience as a nature and canoe guide.

## Mature Value System

Darlene, one of my clients, listed her value system as a strength. As a mature worker, she finds that she is now focused on challenge, relationships, quality, values, and future career potential as well as salary.

Darlene was asked this question in an interview: "Don't you think that you are overqualified for this job? You told me that you were making $90,000 in your last consulting job. Why would you be willing to accept this $55,000 training position?"

She responded, "Of course, I would like to make more than $55,000 in this training position, but I do want you to know that I consider challenge, relationships, and future career potential as well as compensation. I am very interested in this position and am open to your offer." Darlene negotiated the offer *after* receiving it in writing.

---

### Think Before Rejecting Any Offer

If you are truly interested in a position, never reject the offer until you actually receive it in writing. Generally, the offer has negotiation potential. Also, remember to ask about the level of the position. You may qualify for a higher level and receive more compensation. Or you may be able to take on additional responsibility for greater compensation.

---

## Broad Network of Contacts

Your age advantage is particularly important in the career-transition process in terms of your ability to network yourself into an information meeting or interview, but how does it benefit a potential employer? Following is how Shara used this advantage for a potential sales position.

- "In my resume, I will say that my broad network of insurance clients and prospects will assist in accelerated new business growth.

- "In my interview, I'll hit on the same theme, and, without giving away any specific names, I can allude to the number of contacts, industries, and so on that I have."

Shara's experience is a powerful advantage to emphasize in a sales-related position.

## Excellent Crisis Management

As a mature worker in a high-stress industry, Jorges rarely "goes to pieces in a crisis situation." He sees many younger, less-experienced workers refuse to attempt a difficult project, lose their cool, and confront coworkers with open hostility; but, over the years, he has learned self-control and how to defuse tense situations. Here is how he emphasized these skills:

- "On my resume, I wrote that I was a trained mediator, experienced in successful conflict resolution.

- "In the interview, I said that I have successfully worked with difficult clients and difficult situations.

- "My proof was this incident: I was conducting a leadership program for a major airline. During the pilot (rehearsal) program, three internal trainers from the airline constantly critiqued me during the breaks, in the restroom, even calling me at home at night. I was really bummed out and could not perform at my best. They were not used to working with an outside trainer and incessantly tried to change my program and my delivery. My solution was to call the person who hired me and suggest that I could be more effective with one internal trainer critiquing me (her). I asked whether she would like to co-facilitate the program with me. She understood and was pleased with this idea. This move solved the issue, and, when the real leadership-training program started, it was doubly effective."

Two common behavioral interview questions are "Tell me about the time you had a conflict with a coworker," and "Tell me about your worst boss." You can really shine in an interview by describing examples of your crisis-management expertise.

## Balanced Ego

John felt that his balanced ego was a real advantage over younger workers. He was less concerned with title and job perks than with mentoring and nurturing others. Here is how he addressed these strengths in interviews:

"You probably wonder why I'm willing to consider a position in sales training instead of my former position of vice president of sales and marketing. In my experience as a sales manager, I found that one of the areas I liked best was training and mentoring new salespeople. I found it extremely rewarding to train them in the sales techniques that made me successful. I love to see them succeed and reach their sales goals, and I have instant credibility because of my hands-on sales experience."

Having a balanced ego doesn't mean that you have to settle for a lower-paying position or title, but it does give you the right to exercise your career options without embarrassment.

## Self-Confidence Based on Past Successes

La Shay believes that one of her greatest advantages is the self-confidence with which she tackles new experiences. Her confidence is based on past successes. She described herself this way:

- "In my resume summary, I wrote this: Diverse experience in human resources, including recruiting, handling EEOC complaints, designing employee benefit handbooks, and training and development.

- "My proof was that I was recognized by my company for my willingness to accept complex new assignments based on past successes.

- "In an interview, I related this example of my strength: 'I had never written an employee handbook, before. I was excited about the challenge. I called friends who were members of the Society for Human Resource Management (SHRM) and requested copies of their employee manuals (minus the company-sensitive information), and ordered a software program recommended on the SHRM Web site. This was a difficult task, but I had quite successful results.'"

If you recently have been downsized or otherwise discouraged in your career, you may have a hard time feeling self-confident about recent career experiences. You can give yourself a "power surge" by thinking back beyond the recent months.

## What Accomplishments Have You Achieved?

Write down several of your past achievements and accomplishments that you are proud of. Consider all past careers and volunteer experiences.

I. _____

_____

2. _____

_____

3. _____

_____

4. _____

_____

5. _____

_____

# Overcoming Age-Related Stereotypes

Mature workers generally take at least a month longer in their career search than do younger workers, and recent reports from the Bureau of Labor Statistics indicate that workers over 45 make up one-third of the long-term jobless. (The bureau defines long-term jobless as workers unemployed after six months.) Why is that?

I'll turn 60 next month. I just can't see Corporate America wanting to hire an overpriced grandmother as their human resources manager. I'll probably have to take a lesser position and a huge pay cut.

Your age and experience are valued by Corporate America. You have an advantage over younger candidates with your strengths and expertise. You can network at the SHRM luncheon and pick up valuable referrals.

*Negative Stereotype: You're too expensive.*

Mature workers' job searches can take longer for some very positive reasons. First, mature workers often have senior-level executive positions that historically take longer to fill. Second, mature workers often choose to explore different career options when making a transition. Finally, mature workers often can afford to and do take recreational time off between careers.

However, the fact that you as an over-40 worker may be unemployed longer than a younger person can be discouraging. In fact, you may be wondering, "If we over-40ers are so great, talented, and so on, why aren't we hired more quickly?" The truth is that mature workers frequently are both blatantly and subtly ambushed or discriminated against by interviewers (and even themselves) who are harboring negative stereotypes about age. What's worse is that you can unconsciously reinforce these stereotypes in your resume, networking, and interviews if you are not careful. Understanding these stereotypes will help you avoid being a victim of age discrimination.

Negative stereotypes that you may encounter in your career search are these:

- Your skills and education are not up-to-date.
- Your physical energy is low, and your brain is slow.
- You are using this career as a bridge to retirement.
- You will be incompatible with younger workers and clients.
- You are overqualified in experience.
- You are inflexible.
- You are overpriced in salary.

When you see this list, you may be thinking, "This is so unfair. Don't they realize how loyal and dependable I am? I have such a strong work ethic!" The truth and shame is that many employers take loyalty, dependability, and strong work ethic for granted in favor of energy, creativity, currency, and inexpensive talent. Let's face reality here. If you are going to be employed in a traditional corporate job in an industry that is not age diverse, you too may face these negative stereotypes and must overcome them to be hired. On the other hand, if you choose the self-employment or small-business route (see Chapter 9), these issues will be greatly minimized. Read on to find out how these negative stereotypes develop and how you can counteract them.

## Negate the "Your Skills and Education Are Not Up-to-Date" Belief

David was crying "age discrimination" to me, and I thought that he might be right. He had been applying for broadcast-news and financial-management positions without success for about six months when he asked me for help. When I reviewed his resume, his problem stood out like a sore thumb. He was relying on past experience that was not recent and a 35-year-old degree from a major university. His educational credentials had not been formally updated, and his experience in broadcast news and finance was not current.

In no uncertain terms, I told David that he was not being discriminated against. He had an educational credential update problem that he could fix easily and inexpensively as soon as he figured out what he wanted to do. I told David, "Identify the name of the position you're interested in. Determine the credentials, and let's get started reinventing your career."

David continued to network and became fascinated by the position of real estate appraiser held by a member of his Toastmasters club. He investigated the position, signed up for a relatively inexpensive weeklong course, passed the test, was certified as an appraiser, and was gainfully employed within a week. David has been employed in his new position for three years.

Are you reinforcing a negative stereotype by not updating your skills and credentials? If so, don't despair, but review Chapter 4 to find out how to easily update your credentials.

## Counter the "Low Physical Energy and Slow Brain" Image

As we get older, most of us experience some decline in physical and mental energy. This awareness may come in knowing that we no longer want the stress of constant business travel, or the constant pressure to learn new software programs. In most cases, the decline is minimal and should not pose difficulty in your job search.

I can attest to the fact that I can no longer run a seven-minute mile, and I recently saw a familiar face in a department store but still haven't remembered her name. However, on most days, I can do 20 GI Jane pushups and recall names easily. We all resist and would resent being classified as having low physical energy and a slow brain. In all public situations, we can deliberately project energy and alertness. Following are a few techniques you can use to project physical and mental energy.

- Choose upbeat words to describe yourself in your resume, cover letter, and interview: energetic, change-oriented, creative, adaptable, and so on.
- Be current in your self-presentation, adopting current hairstyles and clothing.
- Use color in your clothing to project energy.
- Consciously smile and open your eyes widely.
- Use enthusiastic body movements.
- Sit and stand tall.
- Pick up the pace and volume of your speech.
- Exercise to raise your mental and physical energy.
- Eat many small meals to increase your energy level. (I eat every three hours, snacking on fruit and energy bars.)
- Challenge yourself physically and mentally by learning a new software program, a new dance move, or whatever. (Just be careful with the rollerblading.)
- Plan responses to interview questions that deliberately describe vigorous physical or mental activity.

The projection of mental and physical energy begins with positive self-talk, and then your body kicks in to help you. Before you go to a networking event or an interview, be conscious of raising your energy level. I usually say, "I am feeling energetic and self-confident." If I am having a tired day, I say, "Although I am exhausted and didn't sleep well, I am a pro. I can project tremendous energy for a short period of time."

## Overcome the "Job Is a Bridge to Retirement" Rut

"What makes employers think that we are using a job as a bridge to retirement? Given their history of downsizing and reorganization, why do they care?" This question is often asked by mature job seekers. The truth is that employers often think that we are using a job as a bridge to retirement because of their outdated ideas of retirement age and misconceptions about the competencies of older workers.

Ten years ago, I thought of 55 as an ideal retirement age. I couldn't picture myself working after 55. Now I don't see myself retiring until I feel physically unable to work. However, many younger employers still think of the years from 55 on as retirement years. They still want to hire those who will stay for five years or more because of the costs involved in training and integrating new employees. The employers want workers who are energetic and give the company their best, and may have seen workers close to retirement go into a productivity decline.

I am embarrassed to say that when I was 43 years old and a "hot shot" VP of sales and marketing, I told my husband, "I can't believe that I have hired a 55-year-old account executive. I hope he works out!" At the time, I was worried that he might be a "short-timer," using the job as a bridge to retirement, not overextending himself. I hired the man because he interviewed well and had excellent references. Plus, I felt that he would require little training. I ran into his wife last year, and she reported that he is still working at over 65.

It does seem unfair that employers worry about you being a short-timer when the average job tenure is under four years. They, as well as you, optimistically believe that the job will last as long as you are both comfortable with the arrangement. How can you overcome the "job as a bridge to retirement" stereotype?

- Project mental and physical energy in conversation and physical movement.

- List 10 to 15 years of relevant experience in your resume, if possible.

- Address the issue of your future work plans proactively, even if no interview question is asked.

- Practice answering future-oriented questions such as, "Where do you see yourself five years from now?"

- Despite the fact that you may see this job as short term, allay the interviewer's fears.

- Don't shoot yourself in the foot by ill-timed self-revelation, such as "In five years I see myself starting my own consulting business."

## Dispel Incompatibility Issues

In some cases, we may find ourselves in an interview and feel really out of place because of our age. One of my clients told me that every time he interviewed in a telecom environment, he found himself the oldest kid on the block. He felt like the resident granddaddy. He had a number of interviews but never received a job offer. His resume, appearance, and interview techniques were highly polished and positive, so we concluded that he should eliminate telecommunications from his job search.

Tom wisely switched his focus to an industry we call business-to-business services. Here's why: In a printing company selling printing services to businesses, age is respected as an advantage, not an oddity. My client secured a position with a company providing staffing and payroll solutions. He is extremely well-compensated and feels that his age is respected and valued. Tom addressed the incompatibility issue by choosing a different industry.

Most industries will show diversity in hiring when you present yourself in a way that shows that you are compatible with younger workers and clients. You can proactively crush their false impressions by following these guidelines:

- Dress in current fashion, but appropriate to your age.
- Proactively present examples of recent participation in youth-oriented activities.
- Be prepared to show compatibility in interview answers—for example, describe the time you participated in a multigenerational team.
- Use current buzzwords and industry terminology in your resume and in person.
- Read current business books and business book reviews regarding management, team behavior, and industry trends.
- Stay current on world events, movies, sports, and music.
- Mention interests you have in common with younger people.
- Be aware not to replicate what used to annoy you about the "older generation" at work: bifocals on chains, ear hair, and not engaging socially with coworkers.

## Conquer Overqualification Concerns

Although it seems tactless, interviewers and recruiters frequently ask, "Don't you think you're overqualified for this position?" This question will come as a shock to you if you are unprepared for it.

It's important to understand the real question behind the question. This question can mean

- You have so much experience that I believe you'll jump ship soon for a better opportunity.
- I'm afraid that you'll be after my position next.
- I'd rather have someone with less experience who is more trainable.
- You will probably be too expensive.
- I'm suspicious of your motives.

or

- I just don't understand why you are interested in a lower-level job.

 Wow! So how do you cut to the chase and find out what they really mean by "overqualified"? One of the best ways is to flat-out ask, "Can you tell me what you mean by overqualified?" When you use this tactic, be sure to smile and soften your voice when you ask the question. When you find out what they mean, you can more appropriately address their concerns.

 Other ways to handle the overqualification issue are by using humor, such as "I like to see myself as the best qualified, instead of overqualified." Or, "I don't see myself as overqualified. I just believe that you'll be getting more bang for your bucks!"

Think about what you will say when this issue comes up. Also be aware that you may have created your own problem by listing too many years of experience on your resume. In Chapter 5, I recommend that you list only 10 to 15 years of relevant work experience. Omit your college graduation date unless it is recent.

Also, you may want to consider addressing the overqualification issue proactively in your cover letter or in the interview. I was impressed with the answer from one of my career clients at the beginning of our interview. I was looking at his resume and he volunteered, "You may think that I'm a bit far down the road in terms of experience, but I am excited about this opportunity, and I have the energy and stamina to make this happen." I was so impressed that my mind went from "overqualified" to "best qualified."

Following are some tips for handling the overqualified issue:

- Be prepared to address the overqualification issue by looking for the question behind the question.

- Address the overqualification issue with a positive statement about your qualifications.
- Avoid the overqualification issue by listing only 10 to 15 years of relevant experience on your resume and no graduation date unless recent.
- Proactively address your perceived overqualification in your cover letter or the interview.

## Overcome the "Overpriced" Issue

The "overpriced" issue shares a lot in common with the "overqualified" issue. Interviewers see your years of experience and titles, such as Sr. V.P. or J.D., and jump to the conclusion that they cannot afford you. It's rare that they will say, "Aren't you overpriced for this position?" More likely, they will refer to the fact that you are overqualified for the position.

A very good way to handle the question in terms of salary expectations when you are an overpriced job seeker applying for a lower-priced position than the one previously held is to say, "I value challenge and relationships. Salary is not my sole consideration. I am definitely interested in this position."

You might also ask questions to determine whether you can come in at a higher salary grade based on your experience. Remember—once you receive an offer, you have the opportunity to negotiate a higher salary and even a sign-on bonus. Don't turn down the job before you receive an offer.

To find out how the position you are considering stacks up in today's market values, go to www.salary.com. If your experience leaves you truly overpriced for the position you are seeking, you need to be flexible. If you are overpriced, try to emphasize your value in terms of improving the employer's bottom line.

Use these tips in addressing the overpriced issue:

- Indicate that salary is only one part of your employment motivations.
- Indicate that you have some salary flexibility.
- Concentrate on your fit for the position and benefits to the employer.
- Investigate position levels to increase your salary potential.

- Encourage the offer if you are interested.
- Negotiate your salary and a sign-on bonus.

When an organization wants to hire me as a career counselor or a professional speaker but feels that my fee is more than they can afford, I successfully use this phrase, "I feel that, if we want to do business together, money will not be an issue." This means that we will both show flexibility and work something out. This statement has worked very well for me in the past.

## Staying Focused Throughout Your Career Search

Continue to look for every opportunity to emphasize the strengths and advantages of your age and to avoid the age ambush by muting interviewers' negative stereotypes. Sometimes you have to work around age issues. At all times, you must monitor your self-talk, keep your sense of humor, and look at all your options.

### Work Around Age Issues

Recently, Bob, one of my clients, mentioned his concern of not hearing well in an interview, despite the fact that he wore two hearing aids. He wanted to know how to address this issue if noise became a problem. I can relate well to this because my husband has worn two hearing aids for years. Background noise is a big problem. Batteries unexpectedly going out are another problem. Bob joked, "When you have laser surgery to correct you eyesight, you may end up with 20/20 or 20/30. When you get hearing aids, you hear...sometimes."

Bob and I both agreed that without mentioning his hearing issue, he might say, "It's a little noisy in here. Could we go somewhere a bit quieter?" Or when necessary, "Would you mind repeating that?"

### Monitor Your Self-Talk

Keep up your positive motivation through positive self-talk. I believe that we are ageless in terms of our energy and competency. Some people are unenergetic and stodgy at 25; others are incredibly bright and energetic at 80. Avoid the age ambush by muting negative stereotypes that others hold (and you tell yourself, on a bad day), so that you are free to choose the occupation you desire without age limitations.

## Keep Your Sense of Humor

I am reminded of one of my mature friends in a job search, who got up in the morning, faced her mirror, and uttered these words: "Good morning, you lovely creature. Let's get ready for that winning interview!" Her husband is reputed to have said, "Who is that in the bathroom with you?" It pays to keep your sense of humor in the career transition process.

## Look at All Your Options

Keep this in mind: If you hate having to overcome the negative stereotypes some employers associate with age, you may be a good candidate for self-employment or the entrepreneurial route. The advantage of taking that route is that youthfulness and corporate cultural conformity are not emphasized.

---

### How Can You Avoid the Age Ambush?

Look back over this chapter and the potential negative stereotypes that you may encounter in your career search. Then list the steps you will take to overcome these issues.

1. _____
2. _____
3. _____
4. _____
5. _____
6. _____

---

# CHAPTER 3

## Uncover What's Hot and What's Not

### Finding Careers That Are Financially Healthy, Hiring, and Age Diverse

*"Ah, this is obviously some strange usage of the word 'safe' that I wasn't previously aware of."*

*—Douglas Adams' Arthur Dent in*
The Hitchhiker's Guide to the Galaxy

Where are the financially healthy, hiring, and age-diverse careers? Are there truly any *safe* careers today? They are in industries that are not experiencing recent or consistent mass downsizing. These financially secure employers deliberately seek, hire, and respect older workers as valuable resources because of their practical, transferable work and life experiences; surprising technological savvy; and ability to learn, adapt, and quickly contribute to the company. These employers recognize that the learning curves of experienced workers are significantly shorter than those of students fresh out of school.

### Identifying the Top Five Financially Healthy, Hiring, and Age-Diverse Industries

The top five industries that are financially healthy, hiring, and age diverse and forecasted to be so in the future are

- Healthcare
- Education

- Residential services
- Products and services for the aging population
- Business-to-business services

These forecasts are based on demographics (research on population trends), statistics on the history of mass layoffs, and future career trends provided by the U.S. Department of Labor, the Federal Reserve Bank, executive recruiters, outplacement firms, employment agencies, and my own personal research and evaluation in my position as a career-transition consultant.

## Understanding the Relationship Between Major Layoffs and Financially Healthy Industries

In the past three years, I have participated in layoffs involving in excess of 100 major companies. Although manufacturing, telecommunications, and technology have experienced more layoffs than most industries, all industries will downsize workers and reduce salaries and expenses in response to a need to improve the bottom line. For example, a financially healthy company preparing for a merger or acquisition may reduce its workforce and expenses to appear more desirable to a potential suitor or to have more money to purchase another company. The difference between a financially healthy industry and one that is experiencing mass layoffs is that in financially healthy industries such as healthcare or education, layoffs are unusual, not the order of the day.

Based on my research and career-transition experience, I encourage you to seek a career in industries that are forecasted to be financially healthy, hiring, and age diverse: healthcare, education, residential services, products and services for the aging population, and business-to-business services. These industries do not have a history of current or mass layoffs. They often cut expenses, but rarely reduce their workforce.

You may need to switch jobs in order to find employers that meet these criteria because of dramatic changes in the job market. Two million factory jobs have migrated to countries such as India and China since 2001, and 3.3 million service-industry jobs will move offshore within the next 15 years. Numerous management and white-collar jobs will also be eliminated because of advances in technology and more efficient management.

Although the U.S. Department of Labor predicts that computer and data-processing services will have positive growth potential, I do not recommend them as options for a mature worker. Like the telecommunications industry, these services are not generally receptive to hiring older workers and, for the last few years, have consistently participated in mass layoffs. In fact, CNNMoney predicts that computer programmers and software engineering positions will decline 26 percent by 2015. Other highly vulnerable positions listed on the CNNMoney Web site include financial underwriters, paralegals, legal assistants, telemarketers, travel agents, reservation clerks, data-entry personnel, and typists. Any job that can be replaced by technology or be sent overseas where labor is cheaper is vulnerable. So, I don't recommend that you jump on the bandwagon of a collapsing industry. (The exception may be if you are fluent in Spanish, Indian dialects, or Chinese and are experienced in managing distance workers.)

## Demographics and the Aging Population Present New Career Opportunities

The good news for you is that growth in other industry sectors is offsetting the decline in technology and manufacturing jobs. Baby boomers' needs have added 225,000 jobs to healthcare and social assistance in the past year.

The baby boomer generation, made up of 76 million people born in 1945 and later, is just beginning to enter early retirement years. The future needs of the baby boomers for healthcare and health-related services will be intensive and expensive. They are health-conscious, are projected to live longer than their parents, and, on average, are financially better off than the preceding generation. And baby boomers historically are trendsetters and voracious consumers, willing to spend money on the upper-end products and services they desire, such as anti-aging creams and fitness training. In addition to baby boomers, another 47 million people 58 and over also need healthcare and health-related services and are potential product and service consumers.

A recent American Association of Retired Persons (AARP) survey of workers 50 to 70 years old found that the majority of this age group never expects to fully retire. Their reasons for working reach far beyond economic need, exacerbated by declining 401(k)s, longer life spans, and medical expenses. They want to continue to work to stay mentally and physically fit, to be productive, and to enjoy themselves. Even more surprising are the revealing statistics from the U.S. Department of Labor, which projects that by 2012, nearly 20 percent of the labor force will be age 55 or older. And workers of all ages, including those over 70, will contribute to this mix.

This large group of baby boomers (76 million) and post-retirement-age workers (47 million) will need all varieties of medical, educational, residential, personal, and business-to-business services. Gary, a 60-year-old personal fitness trainer, did a visual survey of the baby boomers at the athletic club where he was employed. He remarked to me that at least half of the 40 and over crowd were recovering from knee, shoulder, and hip replacements, as well as prostate surgery. Gary capitalized on this trend by obtaining an additional certification in fitness therapy. Gary's clients who were not in fitness rehabilitation were avidly warding off the ravages of time with personal training, skin peels, cosmetic surgery, hair transplants, massages, manicures, pedicures, and spray-on tans.

## The Future of Healthcare

My mother, Frances, outlived two husbands; fell in love with a handsome older man, my stepfather, Warren, who was 86 at the time; and married him when she was 82 years old. They sold his house and moved into hers, building their dream bedroom and bath, equipped with a Jacuzzi with handrails and a wheelchair ramp off their deck. We all reveled in their happiness and expected their good times to last until they died.

This past year has seen a dramatic decline in their health, and as their primary caregiver, I have become acutely aware of the upcoming healthcare needs of the aging population that all of us will be a part of. Demographics are definitely in favor of those of you who continue in or develop a new career in the healthcare field.

You may be thinking to yourself, "How can I be employed in the healthcare industry when I need or will need these services myself?" Or, "How can I transfer my current education and professional experience into this industry?" These are excellent questions. As you approach 50, 60, and 70, you will not necessarily begin a new career as a surgeon or operating nurse, but there are many other new careers in healthcare that you need to be open to.

## Don't Make Your Age an Impediment to a New Career in Healthcare

At least one doctor, Robert Lopatin, featured in *Modern Maturity* magazine, began attending medical school in his late 40s and started his practice in 2002 at age 58. If you will still be working in your 60s and 70s, I say why not follow your passion and change careers? My pediatrician, Leila Denmark, featured in many recent publications, is practicing medicine in her 90s.

I'm tired of administrative office work. I would really like to do something different, maybe be an MRI technician. Do you think I'm too old to learn new tricks?

Too old? Girl, you're in your prime! Take that severance package and sign up for that MRI training.

*Negative Stereotype: Older workers are adverse to change.*

Recently, while teaching an Interview Lab to a group of mature career-transition clients, I asked Alphonso, "Tell me about your greatest career disappointment." Alphonso, a client in his late 40s, told me that he regretted his career in IT, because his real passion was medicine. I encouraged Alphonso not to let his age get in the way of his passion, but to use his career transition to uncover career options combining technology and medicine.

A number of healthcare career options don't require a medical degree or physical endurance. Christian and Timbers, a well-known retained executive-search firm, and *Time* magazine support the claim that a future demand is on the horizon for the healthcare careers in the following table.

### Hot Career Options in Healthcare

| | |
|---|---|
| Chief nursing officers | IT and non-healthcare technical managers |
| Clinical lab technicians | Nurses |
| Customer service personnel | Nursing assistants |
| Executives, medical devices company | Pharmacists and assistants |
| Executive vice presidents of sales | Respiratory therapists |
| Human resources executives | Scanning technicians: X ray, CT, MRI |

Christian and Timbers predict a shortage of 800,000 nurses in the next five years. The U.S. Department of Labor estimates a shortage of 679,000 by 2012.

My personal experience and probably yours too supports these statistics. For the last six months, I have been the unofficial case manager for my aging parents. During this time, I have hired and worked with the following healthcare and healthcare-related personnel:

- Administrative and management staff in all areas of healthcare
- Assisted-living services
- Emergency medical services supported by offsite technology
- Hair salons catering to older clientele
- Home foot care services
- Home healthcare aids
- Hospital and doctor valet services
- Meals on Wheels staff
- Medical doctors and geriatric psychiatrists
- Medical and lab technicians

- Medical supply manufacturers and stores selling walkers, lifting recliners, bath transfer benches, and so on
- Nurses and nurse's assistants
- Occupational and physical therapists and their assistants
- Pharmacists and pharmacist's assistants
- Retail sporting goods stores featuring rehabilitative equipment
- Restaurant personnel for takeout meals

You may be unable to see yourself as a doctor or home healthcare provider, but could you see yourself as the owner of a franchise providing healthcare services to the elderly, or as a medical sales representative for the latest artificial knee? How about an attorney specializing in eldercare issues or a property manager of an assisted-living home?

The U.S. Department of Labor and the majority of employment trend research predicts that healthcare will be in the top three future growth industries in terms of wage, salary, and employment for the next six years. A career in healthcare reflects the aging but attractive face of the future.

## Creating Career Options in Healthcare

Chapter 1 presented five potential career options to consider:

- The same position in the same industry
- A different position in the same industry
- The same position in a different industry
- A different position in a different industry
- Concurrent positions in the same or different industries

This is how your options could play out in the healthcare industry:

- **Same position in same industry:** Mary, an employed 47-year-old nurse, voluntarily changes hospitals for an improved environment, an increase in salary, and a $7,000 sign-on bonus, common in today's competitive healthcare environment. John, an MRI technician, leaves a hospital environment for a smaller healthcare imaging facility near his home.
- **Different position in same industry:** Patty, a nurse, takes additional coursework and becomes a physician's assistant. Susan, an emergency-room intake counselor, is promoted to intake manager.

- **Same position in different industry:** Tyrone, a family-practice doctor, leaves the long hours and stress of private practice and subcontracts his services to life insurance companies to perform medical screenings. José, an occupational therapist at a rehabilitation center, leaves to start his own business focusing on elder-care therapy.

- **Different position in a different industry:** Brenda, an experienced nurse, receives her MBA and joins a biolife sciences firm as a research assistant investigating life extension. Luis, a firefighter, obtains a paramedical certification and supplements his income as a paramedic for a 911 emergency service.

- **Concurrent positions:** Eloise, an experienced retired nurse, fills in for nurses on vacation in local doctors' offices. She also teaches art classes at a neighborhood art center. Gerald, a former insurance sales professional, works part time as a pharmacist's assistant and also teaches continuing-education classes for insurance licensing.

All the options mentioned are realistic career changes, which have actually occurred. There is also recent evidence that IT personnel and other managers are migrating to healthcare.

## Exercising Your Career Options in Healthcare

Mina, one of my career clients, had a long, successful career in retail sales and sales management. After mass downsizing at several retailers, she decided to exercise her career options in healthcare. Mina scheduled an information interview at a hospital convenient to her home.

An information interview is an appointment, usually in person, to find out the requirements of a position and the potential for employment. You should interview those who are familiar with the position requirements such as a hiring manager, an internal human resources recruiter, or someone who is currently working or has recently worked in the same position. The questions you should ask, interspersed with pleasant conversation, include

- What are the educational requirements for this position?
- What are the work experience requirements for this position?
- Are you currently hiring for this position?
- What is the salary range for this position?

- What are the hours and conditions of employment?
- What is the future potential for advancement?
- Has this position experienced frequent turnover? If so, why?

An information interview is different from an employment interview. Your intention is not to ask for the job, but to find out if this is a career that interests you. Be sure that you make it clear when asking for information interviews that you aren't asking for a job. For more information on how to set up and conduct an information interview, see Chapter 4.

At Mina's information interview, she discovered that the hospital was hiring in medical records coding and management positions and that she would need to take a course in medical technology and become a certified coding specialist to qualify for the medical records coding position. After completing her coursework and certification in less than a year, Mina was hired for the medical records coding position. Mina is building career longevity for herself and is willing to take a small step backward in terms of salary to optimize her future management potential in the growing healthcare industry.

Another way that you can find out information about a position is to use the Internet. Mina could have looked at the Web site of the hospital under careers or job openings. Next, she could have clicked on the position description to determine educational and experience requirements. In some cases, salary ranges are even listed. Generally speaking, a personal information interview will glean more information, and will establish a positive contact for a future job interview, but the Internet is also a useful aid.

It's important for you to be creative and open-minded as you approach new career options. As discussed in Chapter 1, you may want to make a career change because you no longer have the passion to continue in your former career, or your former career may no longer be financially healthy, hiring, and age diverse. As you look toward the future, I encourage you to reevaluate your career options and to focus on work that is available, is meaningful, and will support you in the lifestyle you desire.

To consider a career in healthcare, you will want to do the following:

- Make a list of healthcare careers that interest you.
- Research salary and educational requirements through information interviews and Internet research.

- Choose careers in which you can obtain additional educational credentials in a time frame that you consider reasonable.

- Look for careers involving post-secondary vocational certifications (certifications that do not require a college degree).

- Seek professional career assistance to determine how you can transfer your education and experience to a healthcare career.

# The Future of Education and Educational Services

At a recent dinner with friends, I conducted an informal opinion survey of products and services needed for baby boomers and generation X-ers. One successful business owner said that an increase in online postsecondary educational services would be a given. When I asked why, he said that because of the enormous expenses involved in college and university education, parents and students who can afford full-time on-campus degrees will be a thing of the past. What he said was true. With more students obtaining their degrees online, educational institutions face an increasing need for online faculty, course developers, and Internet support staff.

## Searching for Online Educational Career Opportunities

Currently 2,500 plus (and some sources say 5,000) colleges and universities offer degrees online. The majority of today's students are computer literate, and the shift to a combination of predominantly online educational services combined with teaching and counseling services is an easy transition for them. The good news for you may be this: You may want to teach online courses. Educational requirements for online teachers are somewhat less stringent than for brick-and-mortar universities. Often a master's degree with recent employment in the field will suffice.

My personal experience validates the transition to online adult education. In the past year, I have seen the online outplacement courses in our career-transition firm increase to approximately 50 percent of our business model.

The online postsecondary education field has a growing need for faculty and course developers who are computer and Internet savvy, and can teach students and develop distance-learning courses. This applies not only to formal college and university curriculum, but also to adult education, vocational education, and certifications. If you have a master's degree or are willing to obtain one, a career as a college or university professor or course developer may be right for you.

## Exploring Primary and Secondary Educational Career Opportunities

The U.S. Department of Education indicates a growing need for special education, preschool, kindergarten, and elementary school teachers, and many states have eased their teacher-certification requirements. More than 2.5 million teachers will be needed in the next decade. Forty states have created programs enabling non-education majors to be certified as teachers after a short course or period of training on the job. Private educational services have employed 56,000 in this field in the past year. The biggest needs continue to be in math and science, and companies are actively recruiting minorities to represent the school populations being served. If you have a bachelor's degree and interest in mentoring and helping others, the field of education may be a good fit for you.

Last year I performed a formal survey of all workers displaced from a major Southeastern energy provider in a period of six months to two years. The surprising common denominator new employer was Cobb County School District in Georgia. Of the five people employed by the school district, only one was employed as a teacher. The others were employed in administrative and IT positions.

There are many positions available in colleges, universities, and school districts other than teaching. A large school district is like a big business. These are the positions I located at a major school district and a large private university with a teaching hospital. See which of the jobs in the following table interest you.

### Career Options in Education and Educational Services

| | |
|---|---|
| Accountant | Food service manager and worker |
| Animal care technician | Human resources director |
| Assistant director of admissions | Information analyst, business analyst |
| Business manager | Instruction content developer |
| Bus driver | Landscaping director and staff |

*(continued)*

*(continued)*

| | |
|---|---|
| Coaches and staff | Medical coder |
| Custodial director and staff | Nutritionist |
| Director of annual giving | Research associate |
| Director of transportation | Teacher's aide and substitute teacher |
| Elementary and secondary teacher | Security director and staff |
| Engineering specialist | University professor, assistant professor, lecturer, instructor |

As with healthcare, the field of education is growing, especially in the online arena, and as an older worker you will be valued because of your education and your professional experience.

## Creating Career Options in Education

This is how your options could play out in the education and educational services industry:

- **Same position in same industry:** Bill, a high school math teacher, leaves public education for a similar position in an exclusive parochial high school. Eli, a headmaster at a private boys' school, accepts a position as principal in a major school district.

- **Different position in same industry:** Judith, a high school English teacher, receives her master's in counseling and moves to a different high school as the school counselor. John, a high school counselor with his masters in counseling, interns in the summer with a family counseling center and transitions into a career as a family counselor.

- **Same position in different industry:** Bridgett, a logistics director for an interstate trucking firm, accepts a position as director of transportation at a local school district. Ignatio moves from director of airport security to director of campus security.

- **Different position in different industry:** La Toya, former sales professional in telecommunications, now sells software to college admissions departments. Wade, a former government agency recruiter, teaches interview techniques to team leaders and human resources professionals in major corporations.

- **Concurrent positions:** Janine works three days a week as a teacher's assistant and two days a week in a different field, retail sales. Kyle teaches summer school in a local middle school and is a guest lecturer on a cruise ship.

## Exercising Your Career Options in Education

Tom, one of the members of my Toastmasters club, was a downsized IT professional with a lifelong love of music. After college he played trumpet in bands throughout the Southeast and then developed and embraced a successful career in software development, capitalizing on the technology boom.

After being unemployed for a year, Tom launched his own one-man band focusing on private clubs and assisted-living homes. This was a rewarding, but not financially successful, move. Next, he applied for a position as music teacher for a small high school in South Carolina. After a successful interview, he became the band director at a local high school. Tom, at 57, is delighted to have meaningful work and to move to a small town where he and his wife plan to live and work in their mature years.

In considering careers in education, you will want to think through the following points:

- If you have a master's degree, check out the faculty needs in your area of education and professional experience for local and online universities.

- Earn a master's degree online while working, meeting degree requirements to be an online professor.

- If you have a bachelor's degree, check out teacher needs in your areas of education.

- Look at alternative routes for teacher certification. (Each state has a department of education Web site detailing local options.)

- Search for non-teaching administrative, counseling, and technical positions in colleges, universities, and elementary and secondary schools.

- Seek career help to transfer your skills and experience to the educational market.

# The Future of Residential Services

According to the U.S. Department of Labor, landscaping and groundskeeping workers are among the occupations with the largest job growth potential in the next six years. You may want to physically provide these services or sell them, manage the crews, design the landscape plans, or create Web sites for these services. Residential services involve landscape sales, design, installation, and maintenance. Other residential services include landscape lighting, security systems, termite and pest control, home repair, appliance installation and repair, cable television services, home theatre sales and installation, and pool sales and installation.

More than 250,000 synthetic stucco homes exist in the United States. The media has forecasted potential moisture problems in these homes, which in turn has produced a growing need for inspection, repair, and moisture warranty services.

I make it a point to interview all my service providers to find out about their job satisfaction, job training, and income. Two of the happiest career moves involved a software engineer and a technical systems developer. One became an entrepreneurial owner of a company providing window-washing services. For the first year, he physically performed the services, but now he expedites his crews and has time to spend with his kids. The second successful career change involved a technical designer who is now repairing appliances for Sears. Neither of these residential service providers has to worry about their jobs being absorbed by technology, migrated to India or China, or being discriminated against because of their ages.

Interior designers and decorators, caterers, personal chef services, cleaning services, estate managers, and so on are other rewarding careers for you to consider in providing residential services.

## Looking Past Your Experience and Degree as You Consider Residential Services

If you have a college degree and have been trained in a specific field such as information services or international business, you may find it difficult to picture yourself in a position involving residential service. However, you may enjoy being your own boss and be able to pay your bills (a winning combination).

It has been my experience that some careers have a shelf life based not only on economic factors such as jobs migrating overseas, but also factors involving perceived age suitability. For example, an over-50 psychologist or teacher does not usually face age-discrimination issues, but an over-50 telecommunications sales professional may be regarded as "over the hill" because of the youth orientation of the telecommunications industry.

Although it's true that executive positions take longer to fill, if you find yourself unemployed longer than the norm in your state (usually varying from four to six months for midlevel employees), you may be chasing a position that is no longer viable in today's economy because of economic and age-related factors. Take this time to rethink not only your formal training and experience, but also what you are interested in and able to do as a new career. You may find yourself realistically reevaluating your past preferences and developing new career flexibility.

Here's an example: I am currently working with an over-40 IT professional who is exploring a career in Christian counseling or natural sciences such as seismology, based on her Myers-Briggs results. She feels that her career in IT is becoming precarious because of economic factors and her age.

---

### Do You Need a Little Help?

Career-interest assessments such as *Transition-to-Work Inventory* and *Self-Directed Search* or the *Myers-Briggs Type Indicator* are excellent resources for arriving at career options that interest you. There are also other useful career assessments available, such as the *Campbell Interest and Skills Survey*, and the *DiSC Personal Style Profile*. For those who prefer a do-it-yourself, reading approach, many books are available, such as *Do What You Are*, by Paul Tieger and Barbara Barron-Tieger, *I Could Do Anything If I Only Knew What it Was*, by Barbara Sher, and *The What Color Is Your Parachute Workbook* by Richard Bolles.

---

The average length of a corporate job is less than four years. Rather than suffer the slings and arrows of constant downsizing, I encourage you to consider residential services as an option. The following table lists career options in residential services.

## Career Options in Residential Services

| | |
|---|---|
| Estate manager | Landscape maintenance owner, manager, or crew |
| Faux-finish designer | Master gardener |
| Franchise owner, domestic cleaning service | Pest-control sales and service provider |
| Installer of pools, ponds, and Jacuzzis | Sales representative for landscape lighting |
| Home painting and repair service provider | Sales representative for pools, ponds, and Jacuzzis |
| Landscape designer or installer | Utilities meter reader and repair professional |

# Exercising Your Career Options in Residential Services

Luis was a former information services sales professional from Peru, working for a major information services provider. His age and the state of the South American economy made his career choice no longer a viable option. Luis was always talented in home repair. After he moved to the United States, he apprenticed with a Miami homebuilder. Later, he marketed himself as a painter, electrician, and handyman through his church and by word-of-mouth. Luis is delighted to have greater autonomy and time flexibility. He feels that his income potential is greater than before. His future plans include incorporating his business and subcontracting his growing business to others.

To consider a career in residential services, do the following:

- List all the residential services that interest you.

- Conduct information interviews with people employed in these positions.

- Investigate average salaries and educational and certification requirements.

- Look at franchises offering these services. You can explore franchise options through *FranNet*, a service that screens franchises and helps you make the right choices.

# The Future of Products and Services for the Aging Population

In addition to medical and residential services, our aging population will need and want numerous products and services. I have selected for discussion a few career positions that are well paying and will always be in demand: weddings and other once-in-a lifetime events, cosmetic surgery and other aesthetic services, and the physical fitness market.

## Weddings and Other Once-in-a-Lifetime Events

Weddings continue to be big business despite the tragedy of September 11th and the economic recession of 2001–2003. CBS Market Watch selected wedding photography as one of the ten most overpaid jobs in the U.S., with wedding photographers charging $2,000 to $5,000 for a one-day shoot plus charges for extra prints. At this rate, diligent photographers who shoot and videotape two weddings a week during high season (May to October) are able to pull in between $96,000 and $240,000 for six months of work.

And then there are other necessary but expensive wedding services such as event facility rental, catering, flowers, wedding gowns, music, wedding planners, and so on. The average wedding today costs in the neighborhood of $19,000 to $25,000, not including the honeymoon costs. Some over-the-top weddings cost in excess of $100,000. The over-40-plus group will be consistently hit with increasing costs for wedding expenses for their children and will financially support and also provide these personal services.

Think about the other once-in-a-lifetime events: Bar Mitzvahs and Bat Mitzvahs; 40th, 50th, and 60th birthday parties; 25th and 50th anniversaries; debutante balls; and so on. What services could you offer to support these consistent and continuing special events?

## Cosmetic Surgery and Other Aesthetic Services

Cosmetic surgery to the face and other significant body parts is big business in the United States, not to mention popular nonsurgical services involving chemical peels, Botox, do-it-yourself microdermabrasion kits, and so on. The most popular cosmetic procedures for 35- to 50-year-olds are breast augmentation, eyelid surgery, liposuction, and nose reshaping. The 51- to 64-year-olds who can afford it prefer eyelid surgery, facelifts, forehead lifts, liposuction, and nose reshaping. As we age, the shift seems to be from sex appeal to appearance appeal.

This entire group favors many nonsurgical procedures. Botox injections rank first place, followed by chemical peels, laser hair removal, sclerotherapy, and laser treatment of leg veins as well as microdermabrasion. Dermatologists and cosmetologists perform many of the nonsurgical procedures in offices, spas, day spas, and skin-care clinics. Many men are having hair weaves as well as hair implants. There are also a growing number of do-it-yourself consumer products that produce less dramatic results such as kits to resurface the skin, encourage hair regrowth, and produce a temporary facelift.

Plastic surgery, nonsurgical procedures, and aesthetic products are big business for the over-40s crowd. You don't have to be a plastic surgeon or operating-room nurse to get on this bandwagon. You might buy into a spa, take a cosmetology course that allows you to give facials, or become a cosmetic surgery consultant who assists in choosing the most qualified plastic surgeon and facility for the client's needs. Does a career in the aesthetic market appeal to you?

## The Physical Fitness Market

Running, biking, weight lifting, calisthenics, Pilates, spinning, stretching, and Burnham hot yoga are wide open markets in terms of service providers, clubs, franchises, products, and so on. Fitness trainers, aerobics instructors, and massage therapists are in hot demand.

You may not believe that you have the physical ability or desire to become a personal trainer at 50, but could you see yourself teaching water aerobics, owning a fitness franchise, managing a fitness facility, or having an Internet Web site selling yoga products such as mats, videos, and CDs?

Recent research indicates that 80 percent of adults over 25 are overweight, with at least 15 percent of children ages 15 to 19 also overweight. Treating overweight is big business, supported by weight-loss supplements and prescriptions, weight and nutrition clinics, and even all-in-one body shapers to improve physical appearance.

In 2004, more than 400,000 Americans joined the ranks of the self-employed. Consultants and contract employers abound. If you have flexibility in terms of medical insurance and salary requirements, an entrepreneurial venture in physical fitness or nutrition may appeal to you. Also, employment at a private club or spa can provide needed medical benefits and a regular salary. Check out the list in the following table for just a few of the career options for services to our aging population.

### Career Options for Services to the Aging Population

| Weddings | Cosmetic and Aesthetic Services | Physical Fitness |
| --- | --- | --- |
| Caterer | Cosmetician | Aerobics instructor |
| Bridal shop owner, manager | Dermatologist | Entrepreneur specializing in weight-loss products |
| Floral arranger, deliverer | Nurse | Fitness facility manager |
| Marriage counselor | Physician's assistant | Fitness franchise owner |
| Minister | Plastic surgeon | Nutritional counselor |
| Wedding photographer | Masseuse | Owner of nutritional shake health bar |
| Wedding planner | Spa owner | Personal fitness trainer |
| Manicurist | Yoga instructor | |

To consider a career in products and services to an aging population, work through the following points:

- Make a list of the careers or products that interest you.
- Set up information interviews with people who provide these products and services.
- Research income potential online and through information interviews.
- Investigate educational requirements, certifications, and costs.

## Exercising Your Career Options in Products and Services to an Aging Population

This is how your options could play out in providing products and services to an aging population:

- **Same position, same industry:** Susan, a masseuse, moves from the Concord Club to the Advanti Club because of a larger client base and a larger cut on the individual massage price. Ron, a former human resources director for a private club, becomes the human resources director for a cruise line.

- **Same position, different industry:** Jody, a masseuse with years of experience, begins to work for a chiropractor rather than a fitness facility. Eric, a volunteer video photographer for a major church, develops a lucrative career in wedding photography. The church provides an excellent customer database.

- **Different position, same industry:** Wallace has decided that he needs to supplement his yoga instructor income. He starts his own business selling yoga products in person and via an Internet Web site and leads yoga-centered vacation trips. Phyllis, a former personal trainer, becomes the successful owner of two franchises involving healthful, slimming nutritional milkshakes.

- **Different position, different industry:** Helen moves from retail sales in a large department store to sales in a wedding boutique, eventually developing a career as a wedding planner. Judith, a retired attorney, teaches water aerobics at a senior center.

- **Concurrent positions:** Brenda teaches elementary school during the week and plans weddings in the evenings and on the weekends. William is a career-transition consultant who develops a sideline as a masseuse.

## Encouraging an Entrepreneurial Bent Through Careers in Products and Services

Many of the careers involving products and services in the preceding sections encourage you to develop an entrepreneurial bent. You must be willing to be a self-starter and to market yourself. Also, you must be able to financially survive the business start-up period and persist in the face of an initially erratic income. In many cases you will also need to purchase your own health insurance. These careers are often viable options for mature workers who have a financial base and health insurance provided as part of a severance package. Careers involving products and services to an aging population are age diverse. Plus, you can get started in many of them on a part-time basis while you continue to work in a more traditional career.

Gary, a former human resources professional turned personal trainer, founded his own business, Mobile Gym. Mobile Gym was a unique concept that brought fitness services and equipment to homes at hours that were convenient to clients. Because he didn't have a specifically targeted local market, Gary found himself driving all over a major metropolitan area and working late or early in the morning. The costs of gas, the hours involved, and the stress of traffic were not his cup of tea.

Gary reevaluated his fitness career and established himself at an athletic club as the facilities manager and personal trainer. This situation was more to his liking because he could operate out of a single location with regular hours. Although he still had to sell his services to clients, he had a convenient source of clientele, regular income, a 401(k), and insurance benefits.

# The Future of Business-to-Business Services

Businesses have always needed to provide services to one another. These services include everything from temporary and contract staffing, to computer repair services, to office supplies, to telephone and Internet services, and so on. Business-to-business services are age diverse. Many are healthy and hiring, and it is up to you to do your homework in terms of finding these businesses.

## Bypassing Age Discrimination Through Business-to-Business Services

Robert, a displaced VP in telecommunications, wanted confirmation from me that age discrimination really exists. He also wondered whether age discrimination was more prevalent in some careers than others. Robert said that every time he interviewed with a major telecommunications company, he was struck by the fact that at 57 he was the oldest kid on the block. Somehow his interviews never led to an offer.

I assured Robert that blatant and subtle age discrimination is a reality. Since 1999, the EEOC (Equal Employment Opportunity Commission) has litigated 130 lawsuits with monetary benefits of 58.2 million granted to the litigants. The average verdict has been $448,000. Additional statistics indicate that older workers generally take an average of a month longer to find reemployment, and a few are never reemployed. Facts support the reality of age discrimination.

In addition, human resources professionals and executive recruiters have admitted to me that they have witnessed age discrimination in the hiring process. Of course, age discrimination is rarely documented. It usually involves verbal comments by recruiting and hiring personnel. One HR recruiter admitted receiving a request for a young, attractive manager, and was told specifically not to consider older workers. HR personnel also have seen resumes deliberately culled out because of age.

Robert was articulate and attractive, but not young. He demonstrated no obvious age-related stereotypes such as lack of energy or cultural misfit, but he was down and disgusted about his employment situation. He said that he felt discriminated against because of his age, salary, and experience and that telecom was a youth-oriented industry. I had to agree with him based on the number of mass layoffs in telecommunications and technology since 2001, and the excessive number of displaced clients I have personally assisted in the telecommunications industry.

Robert decided to capitalize on the predicted growth in business-to-business services. In a bold move, he contacted the CEOs of major business-to-business companies by e-mail to determine their interest in his credentials. The response his e-mail generated was a surprise to him as well as to me, because we generally suggest that a targeted formal mailing campaign has a more positive impact than the more general one Robert conducted. At a career-networking event, he announced that he had accepted a position with Ceridian, recently rated number one in a business-to-business category known as "Best of the Web" by *Forbes* magazine. Ceridian is not only a business-to-business service, but also provides personnel supply services to businesses, another growing business trend forecasted by the U.S. Department of Labor.

## Finding Healthy Business-to-Business Companies

*Forbes* magazine produces an annual list of "400 Big Companies." In its most recent listing were 23 companies representing business service and business supplies. The significance of the *Forbes* list was that the companies were selected based on positive earnings per share and a five-year positive stock market change. The leader for this period was Lexmark, with other notables being H&R Block, Cintas, Emcor, Express Scripts, First Data, and Omnicom Group.

In your job campaign, it important to be proactive rather than reactive, and to choose potential employers who are financially sound because they are more likely to offer higher salaries, bonus opportunities, better benefit arrangements, and continued employment. Robert was able to negotiate a salary higher than with his last employer, and he also negotiated a sign-on bonus.

AARP annually chooses the "Best Employers for Workers Over 50" based on its practices and policies for valuing the mature worker. The business-to-business services listed by AARP include Adecco Employment Services, Melville, New York; First Tennessee National Corporation, Memphis, Tennessee; Lincoln Financial Group in Philadelphia, Pennsylvania; Pinnacle West Capital Corporation, Phoenix, Arizona; Principal Financial Group, Des Moines, Iowa; Ultratech, Inc., Huntington, West Virginia; and West in Eagan, Minnesota.

Look for formal listings of business-to-business services on chamber of commerce Web sites in your area and do thorough formal Internet research by industry type. Be sure to check out a company's financial history. Word-of-mouth recommendations through networking can also uncover some real gems. Having had my own business for 12 years, I have used a number of office-supply and equipment services. When I needed volume workbook reproduction, I contacted Ikon Office Supplies and received a pleasant call from a sales professional almost old enough to be my father. He was charming and professional and we did business for several years. Just last week while participating in a community volunteer activity, I met another Ikon sales professional who was young and happy in his job. I asked him if the company was still age diverse and stable, and he assured me that it was.

It pays to research the business-to-business services in your area and ask yourself how your position would fit in the business-to-business environment.

## Career Options in Business-to-Business Services

| | |
|---|---|
| Administrative support | Human resources support |
| Corporate attorney | Middle management |
| Customer service management | Production management |

*(continued)*

*(continued)*

| | |
|---|---|
| Customer service support | Production line |
| Executive positions: COO, CEO, CIO | Sales |
| Human resources management | Sales management |

## Exercising Your Career Options in Business-to-Business Services

If you are considering a business-to-business service, you can choose from these options:

- **Same position, same industry:** Robert leaves a sales management position at a staffing firm to join a large office-supply company. Judy moves from a customer service position at a purified-water supply company to a customer service position at a printing company.

- **Same position, different industry:** Ricardo moves from a management position in telecommunications to a management position in a linen-supply company. Judith moves from an IT position in a pharmaceutical company to an IT position in a printing company.

- **Different position, same industry:** Lois, a claims examiner for an insurance company, transitions into a successful career in copier sales. Lucy, an underwriter for an insurance company, moves to a different insurance company to pursue a customer service management opportunity.

- **Different position, different industry:** Rich, a tennis pro, transitions into a career in tennis equipment sales to pro shops and colleges. John, a professional speaker who became tired of entrepreneurial uncertainty, joined an international broadcast company as its head trainer.

- **Concurrent positions:** David sells advertising for a local magazine and refurbished printing cartridges over the Internet.

To consider a career in business-to-business services, do the following:

- Research local and national companies for advertised and unadvertised positions.

- Check out the financial history of companies of interest on the Internet at the companies' own Web sites. Look for rising stock prices and positive earnings per share.
- Consider how your transferable skills will apply to a similar or different position in the business-to-business industry.
- Determine what additional skills or educational credentials are needed to make this transition.

## Comfortably Managing Your Transition

It's natural to feel discomfort or fear whenever you are considering a change of position or industry, but there is danger in the comfort zone. The danger is that you may not be growing mentally, physically, and creatively, and your sense of security may prevent you from reading the subtle signals that your company is preparing for a reduction in workforce. Or, you may be truly secure in your position but long to try something new, a career that you consciously choose and develop.

---

### What Careers Interest You?

You can comfortably manage your transition by taking the time to learn more about yourself and your career options.

1. Take a moment now to write down the industries and positions that you want to learn more about.

_____

_____

_____

_____

2. Take a career assessment such as the *Transition-to-Work Inventory* to find out about your vocational interests and aptitudes. Write down the results.

_____

_____

_____

_____

_____

*(continued)*

---

*(continued)*

3. Research careers that interest you through information interviews and on the Internet. Especially look for careers that are financially healthy, hiring, and age diverse. Write them here.

_____

_____

_____

_____

_____

4. Read Chapter 3 for information on the skills and credential updates you'll want to get to qualify for financially healthy, hiring, and age diverse careers.

# CHAPTER 4

## Acquire Inexpensive Skill and Credential Updates

### Revive a Current or Past Career or Jump-Start a New One

*"When love and skill work together, expect a masterpiece."*

*—John Ruskin*

As a mature worker, your career transition shares a common thread with that of a recent high school or college graduate in that you too may be asking yourself, "What do I want to do for the rest of my life?" or "What's next?" But here the similarity ends. You hold the trump card because of your work experience and life wisdom.

Voluntary or involuntary career transition is an opportunity for you to choose the work you love and then to update or acquire the required skills and credentials to be gainfully employed. Based on my experience as a career counselor, the majority of my clients do not want to go back to school for a four-year degree or take out a home-equity loan to pay for additional education, but they are very open to inexpensive skill and credential updates that do not take a lot of time.

In creating a career for yourself, you can choose to stay in the same position within the same or a different industry, take a different position within the same industry, or make a complete change by seeking a different position within a different industry. This chapter looks at skill and credential updates you can get to help you reach all of these choices.

## Getting the Information You Need

One of the negative stereotypes some employers hold is that older workers have stale skills and credentials. To avoid reinforcing that negative stereotype, you need to do some research—regardless of the type of career move you choose.

I need to hire two administrative assistants in their 20s or 30s. Older workers just aren't technologically savvy. Wouldn't you agree?

You know that's not really true. My mom is in her 50s. She uses the Internet constantly, and she is more proficient with Word, Excel, PowerPoint—you name it—than I am. Did you know that 20% of the technophiles are "older, wired baby boomers?"

*Negative Stereotype: Older workers know nothing about computers.*

## Let Your Fingers Do the Walking

To check out certification, training, education requirements, salary range, and costs within a familiar or unfamiliar job position, begin by using the Web. These five Web resources can provide you with information without the time, effort, and expense of setting up appointments with people, getting dressed for a meeting, or traveling:

- Obtain a job description and education, certification, and experience requirements at www.monster.com. Go to "search jobs" and type in the name of the job.

- Check out salary range according to geographical area at www.salary.com or www.monster.com.

- Go to the Web sites of local colleges and universities for information about courses, certifications, and so on.
- In your favorite Internet search engine, type the name of the certification training or education you are seeking, as well as your area—for example, *massage therapy training Ohio*.
- State government employment Web sites provide position descriptions with required credentials.

Buyer beware! Costs and times of credential updates vary widely. Check several sources. Ask for recommendations. Also, there are possibilities for paid internships while you are becoming certified.

## Start Doing Some Talking

Do your research, and then seek the personal advice of someone working in your position of interest. Regardless of whether you are seeking the same or a different position within a familiar or unfamiliar industry, you can embrace the change more gracefully if you follow these suggestions:

- Conduct information interviews with people in the type of position that interests you.
- Consider working in your position of interest as an assistant, apprentice, intern, or volunteer. In your Internet search engine, type the word *internship, apprentice,* or *volunteer opportunities* and your area or location of interest. You'll be amazed at the number of existing opportunities you'll discover. You may even be able to create your own during an information interview.

  The difference between an apprentice and an intern is that an apprentice exchanges labor for instruction and experience and is paid as he learns. An intern exchanges labor for experience, but is supposed to have basic skills in the position and industry. Internships may be either paid or unpaid.

- Consider working in the position on a temporary or part-time basis. Look for opportunities through temporary employment agencies, which often offer free training in computer skills. Many temporary positions develop into permanent jobs.

Get your feet wet before you make a decision. You will have much more confidence in yourself and your decision if you invest as much time as necessary (or you can afford) in researching your options.

## How to Conduct an Information Interview

- Make a personal or telephone appointment at the person's convenience. Make it clear that you are looking for information and not asking for a job.

- Be considerate of the other person's time and be well prepared with your questions.

- Ask about experience, educational and credential requirements, and salary range.

- Inquire about hours and conditions of employment, including hiring, future growth potential, and assistant or internship possibilities.

- Start with small talk to keep the interview from sounding like an interrogation.

- Make sure that you have your resume and business card with you—just in case you have an opportunity to share them or are asked for them.

- Send a thank-you note after the information interview.

## Rethink the Money

Many of the positions you investigate may be low paying compared to your previous salary. You may find yourself asking, "Why would anyone in their right mind work for this low salary or hourly rate?" There are a number of positive reasons why people accept lower wages. Those reasons include

- Time flexibility

- The freedom to hold concurrent (multiple) positions

- The desire to no longer work full-time for "the man"

- To express interests and values, to be challenged, and so on

- The opportunity to learn and progress in a new position or industry

Of all the reasons older workers give for choosing low-paying positions, make sure that yours is not one forced on you by default. Don't allow yourself to be no longer marketable in your former field. Don't refuse to take the time or expense to update your skills and credentials. Take control of your future by using your wisdom and experience to make wise choices today.

## Refresh Your Skills and Credentials for the Same Position

When you are seeking the same or similar position in the same industry or the same position in a different industry, you may not need to update your credentials. If you have kept up your licensure, retained memberships, taken recent continuing-education courses, had current on-the-job training, or recently attended a college or university, you may be good to go.

On the other hand, if you have had no skills or credential updates since high school or college, you will usually need to update your skills and credentials. Updating skills and credentials demonstrates a clear career commitment.

Gina was a Human Resources Director for a major governmental agency. When she was 52 years old, she took an "early out," accepting a reduced early retirement salary to pursue her passion, contract training for corporations and seminar companies. After five years of inconsistent training income, excessive travel, tired feet, and a declining IRA, Gina opted to reenter the field of human resources, but she had let her Senior Professional in Human Resources (SPHR) credentials expire, and she had to take a test to reinstate her credentials.

Now happily situated in a senior human resources position, Gina has no regrets about the five years she spent pursuing her passion. She is remaining flexible as her future unfolds. Gina reminds us all that passions and ideal careers change as life circumstances change.

---

### Think Before You Let a License Expire

When you are leaving a position where you are currently licensed, you should seriously consider maintaining your license and memberships at your own expense. You may want to use them in the future. Although I do not actively practice law, I maintain my license on an inactive status. If I were to drop my licensure, I would have to take the grueling bar exam again before I could practice law.

---

Here are a few examples of job seekers who updated their skills and credentials for the same position in the same or different industry. Notice that some cases do not require formal recertification or training.

## Updating Skills and Credentials for the Same Position

| Position | Skill and Credential Updates | Update Cost and Time | Salary Potential |
| --- | --- | --- | --- |
| Human resources professional in manufacturing: updating credentials, reentering the workforce in a new industry (healthcare*) | Take PHR or SPHR test for human resources certification or recertification | Certification preparation courses are $860 to $1,110 and take 3 to 4 days; taken from www.shrm.org, local colleges, and online | Depending on the position, level, and location, salaries range from $40,000 to $85,000 |
| Adjunct continuing education professor at local college (education*) | Rely on past credentials and experience; create your own course; contact local college or university for details | N/A | $500 to $650 per course. |
| Customer service representative in telecommunications to customer service representative for printer manufacturer (business-to-business services*) | Rely on transferable credentials and experience; learn current industry news, trends, and buzzwords in your research; use these in your resume and interview | N/A | $28,000–$33,000. |

*Industries that are financially healthy, hiring, and age diverse.

## Refresh Your Skills and Credentials for a Different Position

The transition from one position to another position in the same industry is not always a matter of skill or credential updates. Transitioning often involves convincing senior management that you are ready for a position of increasing responsibility, or may require moving to another company where you have not been previously stereotyped. You may have heard the definition of an expert: someone who is from out of town. Here's a case study of someone who made the transition:

> I entered the insurance brokerage industry with the position title of administrative assistant. I had a college degree, a law degree, and years of supervisory work experience, but I was an unproven commodity in a start-up subsidiary of a major corporation.
>
> After a year, I mentioned to our senior vice president that I was interested in a management position. His immediate response was, "What makes you think you have management potential?" And, "I already have enough stallions in this organization." I was devastated.
>
> The senior VP saw me through the eyes of my original position. I reminded him of my supervisory experience, and my graduation from law school, cum laude, while working full-time, but this was not enough to change his mind.
>
> I continued to accept and request challenging assignments and submit original ideas. Less than a year later, the senior vice president sent me on two difficult and highly visible assignments: to start an office in Miami, and to rescue a troubled office in L.A. Dramatic results brought promotions to vice president and senior vice president, and salary increases followed.

You too can change senior management's perception. Here's how:

- Make your desires known.
- Persistently demonstrate your talent, commitment, and new ideas.
- Volunteer for challenging and visible assignments.
- Perform effectively in temporary management positions.

## Refresh Your Skills and Earn Credentials in a Different Industry

Jana was a business analyst in the transportation (airline) industry with more than 20 years of successful experience. She was part of the mass downsizing occurring at major airlines after 9/11.

For three months, Jana searched for a similar position in the airline industry, but no one was hiring. Jana could have beaten her head against the wall, looking for the same position in a currently financially unhealthy industry. Instead, she enrolled in a series of management courses at a local university and obtained a certificate in supervisory management. This educational update, along with her fluency in French and Italian, led her to a management position with the convention and visitors bureau in her state.

There are many reasons why you may want or need to change industries. Like Jana, you may find that changes in the economy have caused your former industry to be financially unhealthy and not hiring. Your position may have been rendered obsolete through advances in automation. Or, you may no longer be interested in your former position or former industry for your own reasons: interest, values, and so on. You may be ready to seek a different position in a different industry.

## Acquiring Skills and Credentials for an Entirely New Career

Where life really gets interesting is in choosing your career transition time to create an entirely new identity for yourself. Chapter 3, "Uncover What's Hot and What's Not," identifies five of the top industries for the future, which are predicted to be financially healthy, hiring, and age diverse: healthcare, education, business-to-business services, residential services, and products and services for the aging population. These industries were among a shortlist selected by the U.S. Department of Labor, as well as top outplacement companies, employment agencies, and recruiting firms.

As you investigate position requirements in these industries, you may be surprised at the low cost and short training time involved in preparing yourself for a new career. I have selected a few representative examples from each industry to show skill and credential updates and income potential.

## Updating Skills and Credentials: Different Position, Different Industry

| Position | Skill and Credential Updates | Update Cost and Time | Salary Potential |
|---|---|---|---|
| Sales manager from sales professional in office supply business (business-to-business services*) | Use functional resume to illustrate leadership experience; take sales management seminar; many are industry specific | Sales management seminar: $1,800; two days | $75,000–$99,000 |
| Former corporate attorney becomes an eldercare attorney (services for the aging population*) | Activate status in state bar association; take continuing-education courses in estate planning | $2,000, including state bar association dues and continuing-education courses; six months. | $68,000–$84,000, depending on employment status |
| Human resources professional with master's degree leaves IT field to become online professor (education*) | Five years of experience and advanced degree | N/A | $3,000 per credit hour |

*Industries that are financially healthy, hiring, and age diverse.

## Careers in Healthcare

Healthcare is one of the top two industries offering the greatest potential employment growth in the U.S. labor force. (The other industry is education.) You can confirm this informally by looking at the employment ads in your weekend paper. Healthcare needs of the large baby boomer and beyond generations are creating a labor shortage that later generations cannot supply because they are fewer in number.

The following table presents selected positions in healthcare with information on skill and credential updates and income potential.

| Healthcare Notes |
|---|
| Make a note of any of these careers or other healthcare careers that interest you. (Check out Chapter 3, and job postings on the Internet and in the newspaper, for more ideas.) |

## Examples of Healthcare Career Updates

| Position | Skill and Credential Updates | Update Cost and Time | Salary Potential |
|---|---|---|---|
| Medical coder | Certificate in medical coding (introductory) | $771; 3 months | $25,000–$28,000 |
| Director of assisted-living facility | Experience managing a business unit; BA or BS degree; assisted-living experience preferred; some states offer certification, such as RCTE (CA) | $220; 40 hours if required | $51,000–$63,000 |
| MRI technician | Associate in magnetic resonance imaging | $1,175 + $605; Two-week class plus two weeks of clinical training | $46,000–$55,000 |
| Geriatric case worker | Experienced RN and one year of nursing management | N/A | $37,000–$55,000 |
| Customer service | Previous customer service experience or entry level | On the job | $28,000–$33,000 |

## Careers in Education and Educational Services

In looking at careers in education, you may think only of teaching, but looking at the Web site of a school system, college, university, or continuing-education facility reveals a variety of different positions, as does the table on page 73. A distinct advantage in exploring the field of education is that most states are experiencing or will experience teacher shortages; positions are age diverse, and teacher certification can be obtained in an accelerated period of time where the need exists.

### Education Notes

Make a note of any of these careers or other education-related careers that interest you. Look at job postings online and in your local newspaper, as well as in Chapter 3.

_____

_____

_____

_____

_____

_____

_____

_____

_____

_____

_____

_____

_____

_____

_____

_____

_____

_____

## Examples of Education and Educational Service Career Updates

| Position | Skill and Credential Updates | Update Cost and Time | Salary Potential |
|---|---|---|---|
| Director of annual giving | Previous experience in fund-raising; volunteer experience can be included | N/A | $36,000–$52,000 |
| Teacher's assistant | On-the-job training | N/A | $16,000–$19,000 |
| Adjunct continuing-education teacher | Subject matter expert, prepared to create and teach their own course at a college or university | N/A | $500 to $650 per one-day course, or course may include several sessions |
| Traffic-school teacher | On-the-job training, outgoing personality | N/A | $10–$20 per hour |
| English as second language teacher | Four-year college degree; certifications: TESOL—Teaching English to Students of Other Languages; TEFL—Teaching English as a Foreign Language; TESL—Teaching English as a Second Language | $695, 60 hours | $1,500–$2,000 per month; many international opportunities |
| Secondary education | Four-year college degree; shortages in math and education; certification times and requirements vary by state | Accelerated, free programs for hired teachers | $35,000–$50,000 |

## Careers in Residential Services

Whether you have lived in an apartment or owned your own home, you have probably gained experience in managing or caring for properties and people. As you observed window-washers at work, you may have said to yourself, "No way I would ever be up on that ladder cleaning windows. Give me my computer in an air-conditioned building." Or you may have said, "That home appraiser job seems 'right up my alley.' My time would be flexible, and I would be outside as much as I wanted."

Let's take a look at a few interesting career choices in residential services and what it takes to get them.

---

### Residential Services Notes

Make a note of any of these careers or other residential services that interest you. What are some of the careers that you have observed in action that you want to learn more about?

_____

_____

_____

_____

_____

_____

_____

_____

_____

_____

_____

_____

_____

_____

_____

_____

---

## Examples of Residential Service Career Updates

| Position | Skill and Credential Updates | Update Cost and Time | Salary Potential |
|---|---|---|---|
| Apartment manager | Apartment management training course | $500 | $28,700; salary can include free rent |
| Estate manager or major domo | Experience managing multiple residential properties or resort/hotel experience | N/A | $85,000–$225,000 |
| Nanny | Previous child experience; perfect references | NA | $10–$12 an hour; live-in at times |
| Mortgage loan officer | Certification given by school, but not required by all | $800; one week | $45,000–$60,000 |

## Careers in Business-to-Business Services

The way businesses conduct business is changing. More and more companies are specializing in producing and delivering goods and services for other businesses and outsourcing many of their business needs: additional staffing, accounting, janitorial, and so on. In the following table, you can see that business-to-business services provide an excellent opportunity to re-create a former position in a new industry or create an entirely new career for yourself.

### Business-to-Business Services Notes

Make a note of any of these careers or other business-to-business services careers that interest you. Look at open positions on a job bank and in the newspaper and notice how many are in business-to-business services.

_____

_____

_____

_____

_____

_____

_____

_____

_____

_____

_____

_____

_____

_____

_____

_____

_____

_____

_____

## Examples of Business-to-Business Service Career Updates

| Position | Skill and Credential Updates | Update Cost and Time | Salary Potential |
| --- | --- | --- | --- |
| Customer service manager | Previous customer service management experience in another industry; could update with continuing-education course | N/A | $48,000–$70,000 |
| Business office manager | Previous office management experience in another industry; could update with continuing-education course | N/A | $45,000–$69,000 |
| Software engineer | Transferable, current skills | N/A | $61,000–$78,000 |
| Human resources manager | Current with certifications | N/A | $60,000–$80,000 |

Transferring skills to business-to-business services from another industry requires unique action on your part. Keep in mind these points:

- Use current and business-specific terminology in your resume. For example, a software sales representative going into property and casualty insurance would describe herself as a *producer*.

- Use correct and specific terminology in your interview. For example, a property and casualty insurance producer interviewing for a sales position in outplacement should understand outplacement terms such as RIF (reduction in force) and migration (used to describe jobs going overseas).

- Learn current trends in your business of interest through news reports and Internet research.

- Create a cover letter that includes two columns that show how your qualifications meet a company's requirements (see the following sample cover letter).

Dear John,

Harvey Toogood, Senior Accounting Manager, suggested that I contact you —— Introduction
about the position of Cost Accountant. As the following comparison shows, my
experience and background closely match your requirements.

| *Your Requirements* | *My Qualifications* |
|---|---|
| Five to seven years of cost accounting experience | Ten years of in-depth accounting experience: Reduced costs and controlled inventory |
| BS Accounting, CPA | BS Accounting, Michigan State, CPA |

(Continue on with
the comparison of
—— requirements to your
qualifications point
by point.)

My demonstrated success in technology and financial environments will aid my —— Conclusion
transition into the staffing industry. I will telephone you on Monday at 10 A.M. to
discuss the possibility of meeting at a mutually convenient time.

Sincerely yours,                                            ———————— End letter

Susan Bethel

*Shortened sample cover letter.*

## Careers in Products and Services for the Aging Population

The final of our five hot career areas is careers in products and services for the aging population, an area that potentially offers great financial rewards. You may be surprised at the potential income of those who provide products and services for the aging population.

### Products and Services for the Aging Population Notes

What products and services could you provide to the aging, often affluent population? Make a note of any of these career options that interest you and continue to be on the lookout for "new ideas."

_____

_____

_____

_____

_____

_____

_____

_____

_____

_____

_____

_____

_____

_____

_____

_____

_____

_____

_____

_____

_____

_____

## Examples of Career Updates in Products and Services for the Aging Population

| Position | Skill and Credential Updates | Update Cost and Time | Salary Potential |
|---|---|---|---|
| Massage therapist | NCETMB widely recognized; not required by all states | Approximately $2,000; certification hours vary by state, averages 500 hours | $60 to $100 per hour; spa takes percentage |
| Financial planner | Certified Financial Planner | $575 per module; each of five modules takes 6 to 9 weeks | $60,000–$70,000 |
| Professional organizer | National Association of Professional Organizers | N/A | $40–$100 per hour |
| Wedding photographer | Photography courses at local college | Beginning course in portrait photography, $89; Apprenticeship possibilities | $96,000–$240,000 |

## Quick-Start, No-Degree Careers

If you feel financial, mental, or emotional pressure to just get back out there soon, these careers may be just what you are looking for. The books *300 Best Jobs Without a Four-Year Degree* by Michael Farr and LaVerne Ludden (published by JIST Publishing) and *150 Jobs You Can Start Today* by Deborah Jacobson (published by Broadway Books) recommend the following quick-start careers for those 55 years and older:

Bartender
Building inspector
Celebrity personal assistant
CPR instructor
Custom closet salesperson
Graphic designer
Home care provider
Janitorial supervisor
Landscape manager
Lawn service worker
Massage therapist
Outdoor wilderness/
    teamwork instructor
Personal trainer
Pest-control provider
Real estate appraiser
Real estate broker
Real estate sales
Security guard
Traffic school instructor
Video producer

Not only do most of these careers often take minimal time and effort to get started, but they also take advantage of the financially healthy industries of residential services and healthcare.

Let's take a look at the credentials, costs and time involved, and the annual income of a few of the practical and the more unusual careers found in the two books.

---

### Quick-Start Practical and Unusual Career Notes

Make a note of any of these quick-start practical and unusual careers that interest you and continue to look for more.

_____

_____

_____

_____

_____

_____

## Credential Updates for Quick-Start Practical and Unusual Positions

| Position | Skill and Credential Updates | Update Cost and Time | Salary Potential |
|---|---|---|---|
| Real estate appraiser | Residential Appraiser certification | $695; 90 hours | $50,000 |
| Head of Housekeeping | N/A | N/A | $44,000–$82,000 |
| Celebrity personal assistant | Join Association of Celebrity Assistants | $100 | $400–$1,500 per week |
| Wilderness team instructor | Intern with Outward Bound | N/A | $55–$125 per day, includes room and board |

## Making a Choice

One of the best things about being over 40 is the increasing avail-ability of future career options for you. Demographics are definite-ly on your side. In the next nine years, the number of workers aged 25 to 44 will decrease, causing a shortage in the labor market, and making your age and experience an even greater asset.

As you look at the number of diverse careers that are available to mature workers, you may be overwhelmed. How can you possibly make a decision? The answer is to narrow your search to two or three careers of interest and do your homework on the skills and credentials needed, including cost, time, and income potential. Having an information interview will also help you make a decision and choose the best source to obtain your credentials.

Take this time to carefully consider your options and choose a career that suits your interests and abilities, and is marketable in today's economy. Make sure that the earnings potential and lifestyle support your needs. And enjoy the advantage that your work experience and life wisdom bring to your career search. Look for age-diverse career opportunities where you can easily update your skills and credentials inexpensively.

### Career Notes

In the chart that follows, create a list of all careers that interest you. Then use these Web methods of investigating the experience and credential requirements and income potential:

- The Web sites of local colleges and universities for information about credentials and education
- A keyword in your favorite Internet search engine
- www.monster.com and www.salary.com
- State government Web sites

## Credential Updates for Quick-Start Practical and Unusual Positions

| Position | Skill and Credential Updates | Update Cost and Time | Salary Potential |
|---|---|---|---|
| | | | |
| | | | |
| | | | |
| | | | |
| | | | |
| | | | |
| | | | |
| | | | |
| | | | |
| | | | |
| | | | |
| | | | |

# CHAPTER 5

## Create a *Wow!* Ageless Resume

### Emphasize Your Experience, Strengths, and Benefits to the Buyer

*"As a job seeker marketing your talents to a variety of 'buyers' (recruiters, human resource professionals, hiring managers, and so on), your mission is to appeal to the 'me, me, me' of each of these audiences. Each has different specific needs, yet all are consumed by one burning question: What can you do for me? Your resume is the first step in demonstrating that you offer solutions to their problems."*

—Louise Kursmark, Sales and Marketing Resumes for $100,000 Careers

"**W**ow! What an impressive resume. This candidate looks like a great fit for our sales management position. Her experience, strengths, and accomplishments seem to be just what we need to dramatically increase our sales and improve our key account relationships. I love how she describes herself as a flexible, change-oriented individual. I'm going to give her a call today and set up an interview." You can expect these positive results from a hiring manager, human resources professional, or recruiter when you emphasize your experience, strengths, and benefits to the buyer and deemphasize your age. But first you need to catch their attention.

### Surviving the 30-Second Skim

Your resume is your sales brochure and should be written with the objective of landing an interview. To achieve this response, you need to create an outstanding description of your strengths, experience, and benefits to the buyer without emphasizing your age. But unfortunately, many resumes fail to survive the interviewer's quick review, which we call the *30-second skim,* and end up in the trash. Resumes from mature workers are particularly vulnerable because they

- Frequently show too much experience
- Fail to show the relevance of past experiences to a new career choice
- Use antiquated career position titles and outdated industry buzzwords
- Fail to emphasize the strengths valued by today's employers
- Fail to use the keywords employers are seeking in candidates

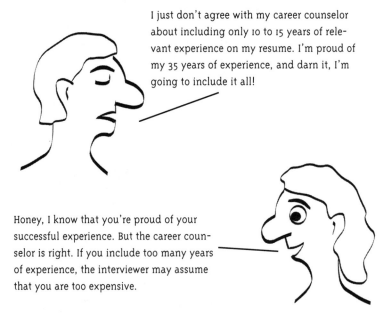

I just don't agree with my career counselor about including only 10 to 15 years of relevant experience on my resume. I'm proud of my 35 years of experience, and darn it, I'm going to include it all!

Honey, I know that you're proud of your successful experience. But the career counselor is right. If you include too many years of experience, the interviewer may assume that you are too expensive.

*Negative Stereotype: Workers with too many years of experience can be seen as "too expensive."*

Here's the reaction to a resume that didn't survive the *30-second skim:* "Look at this summary of experience. This consultant has 35 years of experience. He must be real expensive, and given his age, I don't think he'd fit in this high-stress, high-travel environment. His Objective says that he is looking for a consulting position directing human resources projects. Doesn't he know that we call what we do "human capital management of strategic initiatives?""

I know that you do not want to make the same mistakes our consultant made. Read on to find out how your resume can survive the 30-second skim, and you can give your resume a makeover.

# Attracting the Right Kind of Attention

When you look at a resume for the first time, what do you notice within the first 30 seconds? You probably react to the following:

- The visual impact of the document (the paper color and quality, typestyle, layout, typos, punctuation and spelling errors)
- The heading (your name and contact information)
- The objective (the position you are applying for)
- The Qualifications Summary (your professional work experience)

These four areas must initially survive a hiring manager's 30-second skim and set the tone for a *Wow!* awesome resume that will be read in its entirety and lead to an interview. Here's how to make your resume survive the 30-second skim.

## A Bold Yet Appealing Look

In my corporate career and in my self-employment status as a career counselor, I have participated in the design of many advertising pieces: resumes, cover letters, brochures, and so on. Before I learned to design and produce my own brochures, the graphic artist I employed taught me the importance of eye appeal, which she called "eye candy." To achieve eye appeal, she suggested the use of high-quality paper; high-impact, condensed statements; easy-to-read type; bullets; and plenty of white space (space without type).

A *Wow!* awesome resume shares many of the characteristics of good advertising copy, with a few exceptions: Bold colors, photos, and designs are not generally effective on a resume, unless you are in an artistic endeavor; for example, an artist or actress. Achieving positive visual impact with your resume involves the following:

- Printing on high-quality, classic linen or classic laid paper in subtle colors of white, off-white, buff, or gray.

- Printing in 11- or 12-point Times New Roman, Arial, or Helvetica for the body; 12-point bold for the headings (usually all-caps); and 14-point bold (usually all-caps) for your name.

- Writing in short, high-impact statements.

- Using plenty of white space and conservative bullets.

- Keeping the length of the resume to one to two pages, the exception being a senior-level executive, where three pages is sometimes appropriate.

- Having the text free of typos, misspelled words, and punctuation errors.

## An Appropriate Heading

Never underestimate the visual impact of your name at the top of your resume. Most of us have three or more names, and sometimes they are hyphenated. Just as including all your work experience on a resume may be negative, including all your names and initials on a resume is not always wise. This practice confuses a hiring manager or recruiter and can create negative feelings and prejudice. Look at my name, for example:

Charlene Gail Gilson Geary

This is my full name, including my maiden name. The hiring manager/recruiter may wonder which name to call me and may see me as somewhat pretentious. Here's another way I can present my name:

C. Gail Geary

The hiring manager/recruiter sees me as being either sophisticated (positive) or pretentious (negative). Here is the way I usually give my name:

Gail Geary

This name choice makes it clear that I am called Gail and has no negative connotations. This is usually the best choice. What if my name were this:

Cruella Geary

Although I liked the movie *101 Dalmatians,* this extremely unusual first name may be distracting. It would be better if I used C. Geary.

My clients who have extremely unusual, hard-to-pronounce, or ethnic first names have greater success by using an initial or their middle names.

Your resume heading should include (or not include) the following:

- Your name in bold, usually in CAPS, but it depends on the font.

- Your contact information: your address and phone numbers, including mobile phone number. (You might choose to omit your physical address if it emphasizes the distance of your potential commute.)

- Your own e-mail address (definitely not a shared one), as a hyperlink if sending the resume by e-mail. To convert an e-mail address that is in regular text to a hyperlink, use the Insert Hyperlink icon on your word-processing program's style bar or on the Format, Styles and Formatting menu.

- Omitting your physical address from the resume heading and using a generic e-mail address established for the career search, such as your name @yahoo.com, helps protect privacy and prevent spam during your job search.

Why is including an e-mail address so important? Steve Hines, in his book *Atlanta Jobs,* wrote this: "According to a recent article in HR Atlanta, 85% of resumes now are sent over the Internet. Only 5% are mailed and 10% are faxed. Thus, be certain your e-mail address is formatted to hyperlink. This allows the reader to contact you immediately after reading your resume online."

## A Clear Objective

Have you heard the expression, "Jack of all trades, master of none"? This means that someone has a little bit of knowledge in a lot of areas, but has expertise in none. If your career objective is unclear, those reviewing your resume will not see how you fit the advertised or unadvertised position.

It is always worthwhile to create a career objective for your resume. As you read on, you can decide whether it is appropriate to include it separately or as part of your Qualifications Summary. I recommend using a career objective approximately 75 percent of the time.

Your career or job objective follows your heading and consists of four elements:

- The specific name or type of the position you are seeking. Occasionally two position names are acceptable, such as receptionist/administrative assistant.

- The industry to which you are applying. This is preferred, but may not be possible if your resume has been designed for use in multiple industries.

- A condensed version of your strengths and skills (three is a good number).

- A statement of how you will benefit the company.

## A Concise and Powerful Qualifications Summary

After you've attracted the reviewer with your heading and your objective that closely matches their job opening, what's next? Next is a powerful and concise Qualifications Summary of your relevant work experience for this open or soon-to-be-open position.

Your Qualifications Summary follows the objective and includes the following:

- A summary or condensed version of your relevant work experience included in your resume, usually going back no further than 15 years

- A description of the areas in which you excel

- Your strengths and personal characteristics

## Two Examples: From "No Way" to "Wow! What Impact!"

To understand how the visual impact of the document, the heading, the objective, and the Qualifications Summary work together to create a *Wow!* ageless resume, let's take a look at two entirely different examples: Marie, applying for a position as an administrative assistant, and Richard, applying for a position as a Senior Human Capital Consultant. We'll take a look at *Before* and *After* versions of their resumes and also suggest alternatives that can apply to your individual situation.

### Marie's Resume Gets a Makeover

Marie's *Before* resume really needed help. Fortunately, changing fonts, font sizes, and placement were not as time-consuming or costly as an extreme makeover.

*MARIE THURMOND*
**220 Alta Vista Trace H: (708) 798-1220**
*San Jose, California 30987*
*Mariefoxy lady@yahoo.com*

*Objective*
*An administrative assistant position in a financially secure company where I can utilize my skills in typing, filing and telephone assistence.*

*Qualifications Summary*
*Over 27 years of administrative experience with the same company. Excellent at typing, filing, handling all correspondance, and managing phone requests. Strong work ethic, never sick. Very nice, gets along with most of the staff.*

*Before.*

---

**MARIE THURMOND**
220 Alta Vista Trace
San Jose, California 30987

(708) 798-1220                                              mariethur@yahoo.com

**OBJECTIVE**

An administrative assistant position requiring organization, attention to detail, and strong interpersonal skills to enhance office efficiency and improve internal and external customer relationships.

**QUALIFICATIONS SUMMARY**

Comprehensive administrative experience supporting key executives. Strong interpersonal skills including excellent written and verbal communication. People savvy, flexible team player, capable of coordinating complex projects. Adaptable, change-oriented, "can-do" team player.

*After.*

The differences between Marie's *Before* and *After* headings, objectives, and qualifications summaries are dramatic. The *After* version does the following:

- Consistently uses an easy-to-read business font (Times New Roman, Helvetica, or Arial) and is spell-checked.

- Uses an e-mail address that is professional rather than cute.

- Clearly expresses professional strengths in keywords that an interviewer would find essential for the position and that are listed in a posted position description.

- Uses up-to-date business terminology and current position descriptions, replacing *typing and filing* with *enhancing office efficiency,* and so on.

- Shows how Marie will benefit the company rather than how the company will benefit her.

Marie replaced the verb *utilizing* with *emphasizing,* which has a more professional ring. In the *After* version of her Qualifications Summary, Marie does the following:

- Creates an ageless resume by referring to comprehensive experience instead of listing her years.

- Upgrades her business vocabulary to sound more current and at a professionally higher level, such as *people savvy* and *coordinating complex projects.*

- Mentions strengths that are valued in today's business community; for example, *adaptable, change-oriented* instead of *reliable, never sick.* The *Before* qualities are important, but the wording is antiquated and the qualities are expected.

- Uses energetic language: *flexible, capable of coordinating complex projects,* and *"can-do" team player.*

## Variations Involving the Objective and Qualifications Summary

- For two or more definitely related positions, separate the position titles with a forward slash, as in customer service/inside sales.

- If the name of the position is not clear, use a general description such as "a position in healthcare management."

- In a high-level executive position such as Senior Vice President of Communications, combine the objective with the Qualifications Summary, as shown in Richard's resume next.

- Depending on the position you are seeking, you can also refer to the Qualifications Summary as the Executive Summary or Summary of Experience.

- Using bullets in a Qualifications Summary is optional but can add to clarity and visual impact.

- Omitting your physical address in a resume heading deemphasizes the distance of your potential commute to a perspective employer's location.

## Richard's Resume Moves into *Wow!*ness

Richard's *Before* resume needed help to survive the 30-second skim. It lacked executive presence and currency, and emphasized his age. Let's see what he did to make the resume pop.

Richard and I elected to combine his objective and qualifications into a strong Executive Summary, which is often considered more appropriate for key executive positions. His improved Executive Summary does the following:

- Uses the latest position terminology and keywords.

- Uses the term *extensive experience*, which is ageless, rather than the phrase *35 years of experience*.

- Is specific in industries serviced.

- Highlights specific consulting expertise in the paragraph and the bullets.

- Tells what Richard offers the employer.

- Uses a larger font size (12-point for the text and heading and 14-point for the name) and a uniform and appropriate font (Arial) for a more attractive visual impact. Using as many as two fonts is okay.

- Uses an e-mail hyperlink for the Internet version.

- Uses the more current term *mobile*, rather than *cell phone*.

Be sure to view the position description, if it's posted, to see the required years of experience, but keep in mind that employers are generally looking for no more than 10 to 15 years of relevant work

**RICHARD GARCIA**
rgarcia@att.net
587 Mulberry Street
Cincinnati, Ohio 33957

H: 678-222-9433
cell: 678-503-9954

**Objective**
A position as a senior human resources consultant.

**Executive Summary**
35 successful years of directing human resources projects. Strengths include exemplary leadership and excellent interpersonal skills. Reliable, dependable, and client oriented.

*Before.*

**RICHARD GARCIA**

587 Mulberry Street
Cincinnati, Ohio 33957

Home:    678-222-9433
Mobile:   678-503-9954
E-mail:    rgarcia@att.net

**Executive Summary**

Senior Human Capital Consultant with extensive experience in directing technology software initiatives in insurance, healthcare, and biotech industries. Strengths in team leadership, technology application, and client development will contribute to dramatic income growth and client satisfaction. Recognized for

- Innovative HR technology applications
- Team leadership
- Project management

- Client business development
- Staff training and development
- Critical problem solving

*After.*

experience. Including more years of experience in your objective or Qualifications Summary may cause a hiring manager to conclude that you may be lacking in energy and may not fit in culturally. Also, "too experienced" often translates for them into "too expensive." Why create a red flag in your objective or Summary? You can make your resume ageless by reducing the number of years indicated in your Summary or using the terms *comprehensive, extensive,* and *diverse.*

## Beginning Your Resume

How can you improve on your objective and Qualifications Summary? Don't think that you can quickly complete these tasks. It takes several hours to write a really good objective and summary. Never take the one-size-fits-all approach by sending out a resume with an objective or summary that doesn't match the position for which you are applying. Remain flexible.

If you get stuck, are uncertain about terms to use, or just need a little reassurance, find a comparable job description on the Internet and then alter your objective and Summary to closely match an actual posted position description. Include the keywords found in the actual job posting or a similar job description, in a company newsletter, or in related news articles. When you are finished, read over your work to make sure that your summary is consistent with your objective.

---

### How Will You Begin Your Resume?

Write your heading, career objective, and Qualifications Summary in the spaces provided.

**Heading**

_____

_____

_____

**Objective**

In your objective, include the specific name of the position, the industry, your strengths, and how you as an employee will benefit

*(continued)*

---

*(continued)*

the employer. Writing the objective even when you intend to use just a Qualifications or Executive Summary will help you focus on what you really want.

_____

_____

_____

**Qualifications Summary**

_____

_____

_____

An objective and summary that passes the 30-second skim, is ageless, and creates a *Wow!* impression is always the result of hard work. Powerful resumes pay off in spades but not only in interviews; they also create the potential for a higher salary offer.

## Showcasing Standout Achievements and Accomplishments

Potential employers look closely at achievements and accomplishments. In fact, many share with me that this is their number-one client measurement on paper. In my opinion, the most challenging part of composing a resume is transforming your duties and responsibilities into achievements and accomplishments. But when you do this, the payoff is tremendous. You will have a standout *Wow!* ageless resume, and your self-esteem will go up.

When I left corporate America 12 years ago to start my own business, I had not written a resume in 12 years. I read a number of resume books and sought professional help in composing my resume. When I showed it to a college friend, she said, "Who is this woman? I had no idea how much you have accomplished." My self-esteem went up 10 notches!

As Marie and Richard began writing their achievements and accomplishments, I asked them to answer the questions in the following worksheet to jog their memories about their accomplishments.

## What Are Your Career and Volunteer Accomplishments?

Take a few minutes to answer the same questions I asked Marie and Richard.

Have you

- Saved the company money? How? How much?

_____

_____

- Increased sales? How? How much?

_____

_____

- Designed, created, or developed something original or for the first time? What? What was the benefit?

_____

_____

- Received an award or recognition? Why? For what?

_____

_____

- Been promoted or upgraded? Why?

_____

_____

- Accomplished more with fewer resources or increased efficiency? How?

_____

_____

- Increased production or reduced downtime? How? How much?

_____

_____

- Managed, supervised, or trained a department or team? How many? With what results?

_____

_____

- Managed a budget? How much? Successful results?

_____

_____

*(continued)*

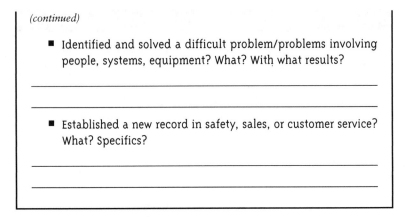

*(continued)*

- Identified and solved a difficult problem/problems involving people, systems, equipment? What? With what results?

_____

_____

- Established a new record in safety, sales, or customer service? What? Specifics?

_____

_____

Hopefully that was a feel-good activity for you that made you see how much you have accomplished in your past jobs or in volunteer activities. Carefully composing your accomplishments will raise your self-esteem.

## The Right Wording

When you work with a list of questions like those in the preceding worksheet, you have an excellent starting point for writing the Accomplishments section of your resume. As you write, keep in mind these suggestions:

- Write a condensed version of your accomplishment as a bulleted item; a sentence or two is enough.

- Begin each accomplishment with a strong action verb such as *designed, led, saved,* and so on, but be careful to vary the action verbs so that your reader doesn't lose interest.

- Start with the result first, as in this example: "Reduced customers' complaints by 75 percent in a 90-day period; promoted to Customer Service Supervisor."

- Although you should avoid personal pronouns, such as I or we, write the accomplishment in such a way as to claim personal responsibility for it, appreciating that others contributed to your success.

- Use specific numbers, achievement dates, and company names to add reality and credibility. (Reasonable estimations that you can explain are acceptable.)

- Make sure that each accomplishment you list will not elicit a "so what?" response.
- Consider each accomplishment a mini-story that uses the STAR approach. What was the Situation? What was your Task? What Action did you take? What was the positive Result?

## The Best Organization

When it comes to writing a resume, identifying your accomplishments is only half the battle; organizing them is the other half. If you completed the preceding achievements worksheet and then listed them on your resume just as they appeared in the worksheet, you probably would have an organizational mess. But how can you untangle them all and present them in a clear manner? I have two words for you: functional and chronological. Both are methods of organizing resumes.

### The Functional Resume

A *functional format* is appropriate in any of these situations: you have broken work history or are changing occupations; you have unsteady career progression; you don't want to highlight your latest employer; or you want to minimize your years of experience.

With a functional resume, you can separate the accomplishments into functions with headings such as Team Leadership, Instructional Design, and Delivery Training. These headings show how you qualify for the requirements of a new position based on your past experience. In using a functional resume, be sure to do the following:

- Group together all of your responsibilities and accomplishments from the same or multiple employers.
- Do not worry about putting the accomplishments and responsibilities in chronological order.
- List your employment information (employer names, job titles, and dates) in chronological order in a Professional Experience section.
- Use functional headings to group accomplishments (effective, but not mandatory). Use up to seven accomplishments per heading.
- Use up to 10 accomplishments from the same or multiple employers if you are not separating them by functional headings.

The functional resume format offers many benefits for a mature worker. It highlights accomplishments and deemphasizes age. If you are changing careers, you can select the accomplishments that point toward your new position. If you are having a hard time identifying accomplishments and responsibilities, you can create five or six instead of having to place three under each employer when you have multiple employers. Using the functional format is also a good idea if you are including volunteer experience in your resume or you have gaps in your employment. In Marie's case, a one-page resume, we eliminated earlier employment situations so as not to date her and used a functional resume format.

### The Chronological Resume

A *chronological format* is appropriate when you have unbroken work history, you are continuing in the same occupation, and you have progressive responsibilities. Your latest employer is highlighted.

## Two Examples: From "So What?" to "Wow! What Accomplishments!"

It's fun to brainstorm and write as many accomplishments as you can think of for each position you've held. Now, let's make it easy on that HR professional who is reviewing your resume.

- Include achievements/accomplishments that are most relevant to the position you're applying for.

- Use at least two and generally no more than seven achievements per position.

- Arrange them with the most significant as the first and last under each position.

- Consider boldfacing outstanding savings, sales figures, and so on, but don't overuse the bold.

- Keep each accomplishment to three lines or less.

### Marie's Functional Resume

Let's take a look at the *Before* and *After* versions of Marie Thurmond's accomplishments, along with her education and skills.

You can see how Marie improved on her accomplishments by giving herself full credit, removing personal pronouns, using stronger and more professional language, and providing specific dollar amounts. If you can't think of 3 to 10 accomplishments, you can

---

**MARIE THURMOND** *(continued)*

### SELECTED ACCOMPLISHMENTS

- I participated as part of a team to plan luncheons, retirements, and appreciation dinners.
- Entered office expenses, purchased supplies, and renewed all vehicle titles, license registrations, and service records.
- Saved 25% by changing kitchen supplier.

### EDUCATION

Graduated—Roosevelt High School, San Francisco, CA.

---

*Before.*

---

**MARIE THURMOND** *(continued)*

### SELECTED ACCOMPLISHMENTS

- Recognized by senior management for effective coordination of luncheons, retirements, and appreciation dinners.
- Handled all details of office budgeting, invoicing, purchasing of supplies, and fleet record maintenance.
- Saved 25% ($5,000 annually) by changing kitchen supplier.

### EDUCATION

Graduated—Roosevelt High School, San Francisco, CA.

### PROFESSIONAL TRAINING

- Time Management (2004)
- Excel and PowerPoint (2003)

### SKILLS

Microsoft Office (Word, Excel, PowerPoint), Peachtree Accounting Software

### MEMBERSHIPS

Toastmasters International; President, San Jose chapter of American Business Women's Association

---

*After.*

change the heading of Selected Accomplishments to Selected Accomplishments and Responsibilities and add significant responsibilities. If you worked as part of a team and do not feel comfortable claiming full credit, use these phrases: "played a key role in," "collaborated with," or "instrumental in."

There was no reason for a rewrite of Maria's Education section. She did not include dates of high school and college graduations, and neither should you. If you did not graduate or receive a degree, use the word "Attended" or "Studies in" or "Course hours" and then the degree program of the majority of your courses. You should include professional training, along with recent dates of completion, showing a positive interest in continuing education.

I recommended that Maria include skills on her resume at the end; administrative assistant, IT, telecommunications, and software engineer positions are considered technical and require technical resumes. Skills can also be effectively included after the Qualifications Summary. For many other resumes, skills are not included in a separate section.

I encouraged Maria to add memberships to her resume because they are relevant to her career objective in terms of communication and leadership. Do not include memberships, affiliations, or associations that have no relevance to your career position or are controversial or religiously affiliated, such as "Member of Brittany Spaniel Club, Weight Watchers International, and Emanuel Evangelical Church." If your interviewer hates dogs, is a skinny Minnie, or is of another faith, these memberships could work against you.

Generally, I would not include a section on Personal Interests unless they are directly related to the position applied for or show exceptional mental or physical energy for your age, for example, "Current International Chess Champion" or "Completed New York Marathon, 2005."

Marie's final resume was this one-page *Wow!* ageless beauty:

**MARIE THURMOND**
220 Alta Vista Trace
San Jose, California 30987

(708) 798-1220                                            mariethur@yahoo.com

### OBJECTIVE

A senior administrative assistant position requiring organization, attention to detail, and strong interpersonal skills to enhance office efficiency and improve internal and external customer relationships.

### QUALIFICATIONS SUMMARY

Comprehensive administrative experience supporting key executives. Strong interpersonal skills including excellent written and verbal communication. People savvy, flexible team player, capable of coordinating complex projects. Adaptable, change-oriented, "can-do" team player.

### SELECTED ACCOMPLISHMENTS AND RESPONSIBILITIES

- Expertly handled all administrative support responsibilities for president of major retail distribution center.
- Recognized by senior management for effective coordination of luncheons, retirements, and appreciation dinners.
- Handled all details of office budgeting, invoicing, purchasing of supplies, and fleet record maintenance.
- Saved 25% ($5,000 annually) by changing kitchen supplier.
- Praised for tactful interpersonal skills.
- Entrusted with the management of sensitive financial and personnel information.

### PROFESSIONAL EXPERIENCE

Value Mart, San Jose, CA                                  1990–2004
*Senior Executive Administrative Assistant*
*Administrative Assistant/Distribution*

Maritime Oil, Houston, Texas                             1988–1990
*Executive Secretary*

### EDUCATION

Diploma, Roosevelt High School, San Francisco, CA

### PROFESSIONAL TRAINING

- Time Management (2004)
- Excel and PowerPoint (2003)

### SKILLS

Microsoft Office (Word, Excel, PowerPoint), Peachtree Accounting Software

### MEMBERSHIPS

Toastmasters International; President, San Jose chapter of American Business Women's Association.

*Marie's final resume.*

## Richard's Chronological Resume

Now let's take a look at Richard's achievements as part of his chronological resume. Richard and I selected a chronological format because of his consistent pattern of work history and because we could easily drop off an earlier employer. In a chronological resume, accomplishments are listed after each employer under Professional Experience.

The change we made to the first achievement involved adding specifics: the name of the software, the client, and the project scope. We used a strong action verb, *acknowledged*, preceded by a strong adverb, *formally*. Additionally, the mention of an HR technology application and team leadership is consistent with the Executive Summary. We agreed that additional Professional Experience should follow, with two to seven accomplishments under each employer. For Richard, the Professional Certifications and Professional Affiliations areas enhance his resume because of their career relevance.

Following is Richard's *Wow!* ageless consulting resume. This resume, like Rome, was certainly not built in one day. It was crafted with professional help and represents about 16 hours of work on Richard's part. A resume will continue to be a work in progress for you; however, the results of a well-crafted resume are worth the effort.

**RICHARD GARCIA** *(continued)*

**Professional Experience**

Andrews Consulting, Washington, D.C. 1993-2004
*Senior Consultant*  Responsible for PeopleSoft applications over a two-year period. Client was happy that we came in on time and under budget. Trained and managed all consultants in the Northeast Region.

*Before.*

## RICHARD GARCIA (continued)

### Professional Experience

Andrews Consulting, Washington, DC                    1993–2004
*Senior Consultant*

- Formally acknowledged by Capitol Insurance Group and by Andrews for leading effective, custom installation of PeopleSoft program nationwide.

- Recognized as key player in $10 million income growth for NE Region in 2004 because of effective training and management of 60 consultants and associates.

### Education

BS, Business, University of Maryland
MBA, George Washington University

### Professional Certifications

FSA; PeopleSoft Certification: PMI Certification

### Professional Affiliations

DC Insurance Institute; Outgoing president of SHRM (Society for Human Resource Management)

*After.*

**RICHARD GARCIA**

rgarcia@att.net
587 Mulberry Street
Cincinnati, OH 33957

Home: 678-222-9433
Mobile: 678-503-9954

### Executive Summary

A position as a Senior Human Capital Consultant. Extensive experience in directing technology software initiatives in the insurance, healthcare, and biotech industries. Strengths in team management, technology application, and client development will contribute to income growth and client satisfaction. Exceptional expertise in

- Innovative HR technology applications
- Team leadership
- Project management
- Organizational development
- Staff training and development
- Critical problem solving

### Professional Experience

Andrews, Washington, DC                           1993–2004
*Senior Consultant, Practice Leader*

- Formally acknowledged by Capitol Insurance Group and Andrews for leading effective, custom installation of PeopleSoft program nationwide.
- Recognized as key player in $10 million income growth for NE Region in 2004 because of successful training and management of 60 consultants and associates.
- Effectively identified and analyzed client issues and handled consulting projects from proposal to conclusion.
- Designed and implemented original training program for interns and associates.
- Selected by Andrews as Consultant of the Year in 1996, 1997, 2000, 2003.

McKinsey and Company, Boston, MA                           1991–1993
*Consultant, HRIS Practice*

- Managed book of $750,000 HRIS clients (Human Resource Information Services) in the healthcare, insurance, and biotech industries.
- Developed $250,000 in additional business with existing clients.
- Played key role in client retention by informing clients and company of state-of-the-art insurance and risk-management concepts.
- Served as adjunct professor in Risk Management at Boston University.

### Education

BS, Business, University of Maryland
MBA, George Washington University

### Professional Certifications

FSA; PeopleSoft Certification: PMI Certification

### Professional Affiliations

DC Insurance Institute
Society for Human Resource Management (SHRM), outgoing president

*Richard's final resume.*

Let's review the features of the two types of resume formats: Marie's functional resume and Richard's chronological one. Remember that you can use skills, professional certifications, and affiliations on either resume format.

## Features of Two Resume Formats

| Functional Resume | Chronological Resume |
| --- | --- |
| Name, address, phone, e-mail | Name, address, phone, e-mail |
| Objective (in most cases) | Objective (in most cases) |
| Qualifications Summary | Qualifications Summary |
| Selected Accomplishments (placed under a functional area of expertise if desired) | Professional Experience (including selected accomplishments) |
| Professional Experience | Education/Professional Training |
| Education/Professional Training | Military Service (optional) |
| Military Service (optional) | |

## Finishing Your Resume

Now it's time for you to write *your* accomplishments. To make them interesting, vary your action verbs. If you find yourself using the same verbs, highlight the overused verb and look under Tools, Language, and Thesaurus in your word-processing software and then choose a synonym (a word meaning the same thing) to replace it. If you prefer, you can use a hard-copy dictionary or thesaurus for the same purpose. The following table gives a short list of action verbs for you to use.

## Examples of Action Verbs

| | | | | |
| --- | --- | --- | --- | --- |
| Achieved | Controlled | Exceeded | Increased | Motivated |
| Approved | Corrected | Engineered | Improved | Negotiated |
| Arranged | Created | Forecasted | Initiated | Organized |
| Assembled | Decreased | Generated | Invented | Procured |
| Budgeted | Directed | Hired | Led | Received |
| Conducted | Edited | Identified | Managed | Recognized |

Use the STAR approach when writing your accomplishments. The STAR approach is a method of telling the story of an accomplishment involving the **S** (situation) or **T** (task), the **A** (the action you took), and the **R** (the positive results). Marie used this method in writing her achievements. For example, she wrote this: "Saved 25% ($5,000 annually) by changing kitchen supplier." Marie put the results first, followed by the action she took. The Situation or Task was understood in her statement, but it also can be expressed in more detail.

Implement these tips as you write your accomplishments:

- Use strong action verbs, varying the verbs.
- Avoid pronouns.
- Put the results first, if possible.
- Give details and specifics, such as numbers and percentages.
- Give each accomplishment the "so what?" test: Will the accomplishment *Wow!* the interviewer?
- Accept responsibility for your major contributions.
- Occasionally intersperse important responsibilities that do not seem to be full accomplishments.

  Example: Managed high volume of travel/meeting arrangements for three executives.

## How Will You Finish Your Resume?

Write three of your accomplishments. Leave the unnumbered lines empty for now.

1. _____

_____

_____

2. _____

_____

_____

3. _____

_____

_____

Now go back and confirm that each accomplishment follows the guidelines recommended earlier in this chapter. If it doesn't, revise it to make it *Wow!* your resume audience.

Add your Professional Experience, Education, Professional Training, Military Experience, Skills, Professional Credentials, and Professional Memberships or Affiliations if applicable.

**Professional Experience**

_____

_____

_____

**Education**

_____

_____

_____

**Professional Training**

_____

_____

_____

**Military Experience**

_____

_____

_____

**Skills**

_____

_____

_____

**Professional Credentials**

_____

_____

_____

**Professional Memberships or Affiliations**

_____

_____

_____

Now you have created the important elements of a *Wow!* ageless resume. When you take a look at your final resume, ask yourself the following questions:

- Does my resume create a strong, positive visual impact: enough white space, quality paper stock, appropriate font size and type style, and appropriate use of bullets? And, of course, does it contain no typos, or spelling or punctuation errors?

- Have I chosen the best format—chronological, functional, or combination—to present my strengths?

- Have I stated a clear objective that matches the employer's position description, separately or in the Summary?

- Have I created a dynamic Summary of Experience that highlights my experience and strengths?

- Will my resume survive the "30-second skim"?

- Does my resume highlight my accomplishments and deemphasize my age?

- Are my accomplishments dynamic, and do they support my objective?

- Will my resume cause the interviewer to say *"Wow!"*?

Don't forget that many resources are available to help you with writing a resume, but you are the heart of it. A resume consultant or software program, for example, can provide you with an attractive format, but you must supply the dynamic information. Career consultants and well-written resume guides such as *Résumé Magic,* by Susan Britton Whitcomb, and *Gallery of Best Resumes,* by David Noble (both published by JIST), as well as *Resume Power,* by Tom Washington (Mount Vernon Press), can guide you in appropriate language and phraseology. And don't forget that there are specialized resume books for technical, sales, healthcare, and numerous other types of career positions.

Sometimes it pays to be different. There are always exceptions to the resume protocol I have covered. I have erred on the side of conservatism because I want you to stand out positively, not negatively. Having said this, I give you license to add your own individual resume touches: an unusual font, showing 20 years of experience rather than 15, using a hybrid version of the functional and chronological formats, and so on. Just be tasteful and have a professional you trust check your resume.

# Getting Your Resume into the Hands of a Hiring Manager or Human Resources Professional

Now that you have a *Wow!* ageless resume, what is the best way to get your resume into the hands of a hiring professional? Absolutely the best way to deliver your resume is to have a networking contact or executive recruiter hand-deliver it or e-mail it to the hiring professional with their recommendation. Delivering your resume this way assures that it will not get lost in the pile of 500 resumes that are sent in through a heavily used Web site such as Monster.com.

The next best practice is to send your resume by standard mail to the hiring manager with a dynamic cover letter, unless company instructions require that your resume be sent in a text-only version through their Web site. In this case, follow the Web site instructions, but also have your networking contact put in a good word for you after you have submitted your resume. Because the majority of resumes are delivered electronically, yours will stand out when it is delivered with a personal touch that separates you from the crowd.

## Trends in Electronic Resumes and Portfolios

We are all old enough to know that following faddish trends is for the birds. However, we are also old enough to be flexible to dynamic new ideas. If a trend is critical to your success, you'd better do your best to hop onboard. That is especially true when you're getting a job in a competitive field. Electronic resumes and portfolios need to be part of your vocabulary and expertise.

After you complete your *Wow!* ageless resume, you should also create a hybrid version of your resume, which is called an *electronic* (ASCII text-only format) resume. The electronic resume is scannable and is easy to create.

### Text-Only Resumes

The text-only resume is basically a block version of your resume without any formatting. Here are easy instructions for creating an electronic resume for employer scanning, sending by e-mail, and posting online.

1. In your word processor, select File, Save As. Then choose text only with line breaks from the Save as Type: list. Close the file.

2. Reopen your electronic resume and left-align all text, including all heading information.

3. Check to be sure that text lines are no more than 65 characters or 6.5 inches long.

4. Move extra characters down to the next line.

5. When bullets appear as question marks, replace them with asterisks or dashes.

6. Delete name and heading information from the second page and move up the text.

7. Check for tabs, columns, or tables that are not in correct order.

8. Correct broken lines and spacing errors.

9. Avoid italics, underlining, boldfacing, varied fonts, and colored paper.

This electronic resume takes less than 30 minutes to convert and check, and gives you a competitive edge in an online job search.

In most cases, an employer or job portal will advise you when to send a text-only resume, also called ASCII. Ask when in doubt. If sites ask for a "scannable" resume, send your electronic resume by e-mail if that's an option. Scanning machines can misinterpret a hard copy.

## Make Your Resume Scannable

You might have heard that many companies require "scannable" resumes. Using scanning technology, your resume is entered into the company database, which the company uses to search for candidates who match specific job qualifications. For the company to find a match, your resume must do the following:

1. **Contain the right words that match the employer's queries (known as "keywords").** Keywords are simply words that an employer or company uses to define the most important qualifications for a job they're trying to fill. Keywords typically are nouns ("sales," "accounting," "customer satisfaction," "Bachelor's degree") rather than verbs ("increased," "achieved," "initiated") or adjectives ("successful," "excellent," "dynamic").

If you have held jobs similar to the one you're seeking, your resume probably contains the right keywords. You can learn more keywords from job descriptions for similar jobs, and you might want to add some of these to your resume to increase your chances of being "found" in a keyword search.

If you are looking for a position unlike anything you've ever done before, your resume might not be found by a keyword search. But if this is your circumstance, you're probably not looking for a job by these mass-application means, anyway.

2. **Be able to be read by scanning software.** What is considered "scannable" can vary dramatically from company to company. Advanced scanning software can read a variety of formats and font variations, but simple scanners will have trouble with anything out of the ordinary. For best results, use a simple, unadorned format, eliminate bold and italic type, remove bullets, and eliminate graphics. Place all text at the left margin, and use at least 11-point type.

You can remove all potential scanning problems by sending your resume electronically, by e-mail or through a Web site application form. Your text or word-processed resume can enter the database directly, without having to pass through a physical scan.

And if you prefer to send a hard-copy resume to be scanned, simply use the text-only version of your resume. It is 100 percent scannable.

## Resume Portfolios

Recent trends to make your *Wow!* resume stand out from the crowd are to make it a part of a hard copy portfolio placed in an attractive presentation folder or as a Web page online. My take on the Web page is that this is a cool idea if you are currently employed or unemployed with financial reserves, Internet savvy, and have plenty of time to be creative in your job search. If this does not fit you, don't embrace this idea. I have written the language in HTML for my Web site, and I can attest to the fact that this is very time-consuming.

On the other hand, creating a hard-copy resume portfolio is not time-consuming and makes your resume stand out from the crowd.

I recently helped Sam, a CAD designer (a creator of architectural renderings for engineers and architects) create a hard-copy resume portfolio that consisted of the following:

- A black glossy pocket portfolio purchased at an office-supply store
- His attractive business card
- His *Wow!* resume
- Colored samples of his design renderings

We produced a targeted mailing of 50 major architectural and engineering firms. Whenever Sam called to request an interview, he was always positively recognized. The recruiter or hiring manager never trashed his resume portfolio, and yes, he was soon employed.

You may ask yourself, "What could I include in a resume portfolio? I'm no graphic designer." Well, you can include letters of recommendation, awards, published articles, success stories from your work experience, and any exceptional work samples.

---

### What Do You Need to Do to Create Your Resume?

Look back over this chapter and make a few notes below on what you need to do now to create a *Wow!* ageless resume.

_____

_____

_____

---

# CHAPTER 6

## Find Age-Diverse Job Opportunities
### Strategic Searches Online and Off

*"You're alive. Do something. The directive in life, the moral imperative was so uncomplicated. It could be expressed in single words, not complete sentences. It sounded like this. Look. Listen. Choose. Act."*

—*Barbara Hall*, A Summons to New Orleans

Job opportunities abound when you look and listen. The fun begins in choosing which of the job search techniques to use. Read on and find out about the merits of off- and online searches and why career counselors recommend using multiple search methods.

"Don't put all of your eggs in one basket" is part of the wisdom available to you as a mature job seeker. And if you want to shorten your job search and increase your chances of landing a job, "put many eggs in many different baskets." What this means to you in your career search is that if you employ more than one job search method and increase the number of daily contacts to prospective hiring managers and networking contacts, you will exponentially increase the odds of a faster and more fruitful job search.

Networking, strategic mailing and calling, posting your resume on company Web sites and on selected job search portals, answering newspaper ads, and working with personnel agencies and retained search firms and executive recruiters are all effective job search methods. In this chapter, you'll find a wealth of information about each method.

# Networking Your Way to a Job

*"The percentage of jobs found through networking is about 60 to 80 percent or even higher, according to studies conducted by out-placement firms, executive search firms, and the U.S. Department of Labor."*

—Networking for Job Search and Career Success,
Michelle Tullier, Ph.D. (JIST Publishing)

Networking in the job search process means formally or informally letting as many people as possible know that you are in the market for a new job. Some people grimace when they hear the word *networking*, thinking that it means going to a formal networking event and talking to strangers. The good news for you is that networking is often just talking to your friends and normal day-to-day contacts about what is going on in their lives and yours.

## Why Should You Network?

There are a number of excellent reasons for networking your way into an interview, in addition to the fact that many experts agree that the majority of jobs are landed through networking.

- As a mature client, your advantage is that you have more networking contacts than younger workers. You have former work colleagues, friends, neighbors, relatives, professional associations, clubs, religious organizations, and so on. And, you can also network with strangers at formal networking and association events.

- Networking uncovers unadvertised jobs that represent at least 70 percent of open or soon-to-be-open positions. In order to expand my career consulting business, I networked with a friend at Toastmasters and was referred to Right Management. Right Management did not need to post their job opening. Their position was unadvertised. I uncovered it through networking and subsequently landed an interview and an adjunct position on their career consulting staff.

- Obtaining a job referral through networking usually increases your value in the eyes of the hiring manager.

- Networking allows your name and resume to go directly to the hiring manager and cuts through the often time-consuming and interview-killing screening or scanning process.

- Many positions are posted on company bulletin boards, which networking contacts can access.

The following illustrations show the difference between networking and responding to an Internet or newspaper ad.

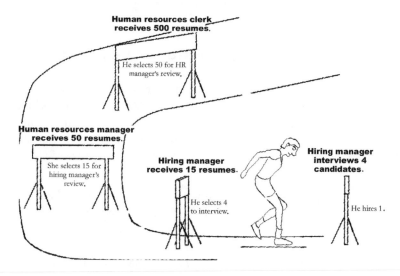

**Human resources clerk receives 500 resumes.**

He selects 50 for HR manager's review.

**Human resources manager receives 50 resumes.**

She selects 15 for hiring manager's review.

**Hiring manager receives 15 resumes.**

He selects 4 to interview.

**Hiring manager interviews 4 candidates.**

He hires 1.

*Responding to a job posting over the Internet or in the newspaper.*

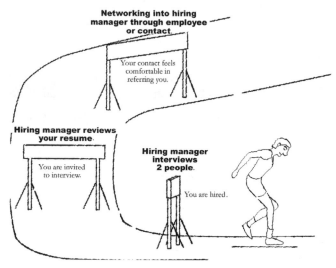

**Networking into hiring manager through employee or contact.**

Your contact feels comfortable in referring you.

**Hiring manager reviews your resume.**

You are invited to interview.

**Hiring manager interviews 2 people.**

You are hired.

*Networking your way into an interview.*

You can easily see that networking your way into an interview often delivers your resume directly to the hiring manager. Even if it goes through human resources first, it does not ride in with 499 other resumes. Your resume is given priority because it comes with a referral. It will have even greater credibility if you can persuade your network contact to hand-deliver or attach your resume to a referral e-mail message to the hiring manager.

## How Can You Identify Networking Contacts?

As I finished Judy's resume, I asked her how she planned to network. She groaned and said, "I don't think that I have any networks. I have been working at Acme for 20 years. When I wasn't working, I was a full-time mom. I wish I had a Rolodex full of names, but I thought I would retire with Acme. I don't know if I can network. I am somewhat introverted. I can't see myself going to these formal networking events."

Judy's feelings are normal. Many career clients recoil when they hear that they need to network. Networking has the bad rap of being associated with going to meetings and social gatherings where you are forced to "network" with 20 strangers in one hour. I assured Judy that she had more networks than she knew and that networking is a normal daily occurrence. "Once you know what to say about leaving Acme and what you plan to do next, you will find yourself unconsciously networking on a daily basis," I told her.

I presented Judy with the following chart and asked her to write down the names of people that she could contact with ease within the next month.

### Who Do You Know?

List one or more people you know in each category that you either normally have interaction with or would be willing to contact within the next month.

| Type of Contact | Name, phone number, and e-mail | Results |
| --- | --- | --- |
| Relatives | | |
| Friends | | |

Club membership director

Club members

Neighbors

Former employers

Former colleagues

Vendors

School/college friends

Clergy

Common-interest groups

Professional associations

Competitors

Clients

## What Do You Say When You're Networking?

Networking contacts are worth calling or e-mailing when you know what to say. Let's take a look at an effective script. Judy agreed to call a former coworker at Acme who had joined a competitor two years earlier.

- **Identify yourself and give the person a memory connection:** "John, this is Judy Forester. We used to work together at Acme. I was the IT manager. Do you have a moment?"

- **Ask how he or she is doing:** "Are you enjoying your work at Write Image?" (If you were networking with a stranger at a business meeting, you might ask, "Did you enjoy the speaker?")

- **Ask about his or her career:** "Are you in human resources now?" (You might ask a stranger this: "What do you do for a living?") Be polite, listen, and show interest in the other person.

- **Tell him or her about your job situation:** "As you may have heard, Acme has gone through a recent reorganization, and I'm taking this time to explore opportunities as an IT manager with another firm." Or "I'm currently transitioning from IT management to e-learning design. I'm looking for a position as an e-learning course designer."

- **Take time to pause:** At this point, your networking partner will probably ask you a few questions and may provide a referral for you. If not, you can say, "Does your company have any opportunities in this area? Who may I contact?" If this does not work out, explore opportunities outside his or her company by asking, "Do you know of any opportunities with your clients or vendors?"

- **Close when comfortable:** "John, I really enjoyed talking with you. I'll call you tomorrow to get the name and phone number of your IT contact. I really appreciate your time." When you call back, ask for a referral, and if you feel comfortable, ask your contact to deliver or forward your resume with a referral.

## Networking Do's and Don'ts

| Do | Don't |
|---|---|
| Have a clear objective: to obtain a referral. | Be overaggressive; do show interest in your networking partner first. |
| Be brief and considerate of the person's time. Ask whether this is a good time to talk. | Force conversation if the person is extremely busy. |
| Have a business card announcing your new career objective. | Immediately hand them your resume. |
| Take the initiative to follow up on the contact. | Expect your networking partner to take the initiative. |
| Ask the person if you may use his or her name as a referral. | Fail to thank them and let them know of your progress. |
| After establishing rapport, ask them to deliver or forward your resume. | Impose on a stranger until you build rapport and the person is no longer a stranger. |

## Strategic Mailing and Calling Campaigns

I recently sent out this e-mail to past participants in my "Age as an Advantage" class. "Greetings. It has been nearly a year since we were together. I would love to hear from you. I am looking for success stories in the area of strategic searches off- and online."

I received the following e-mail from Richard: "Gail, I sent out 1,000 targeted letters to industries in cities and states where I was willing to live and received a 10 percent positive rate of response. You can call me next Tuesday or Thursday between 9:00 and 11:00 a.m. and I'll share what I learned." I was intrigued by Dick's e-mail and interested to learn about how he conducted his strategic mailing and calling campaign. Read on to find out what he did. But first, read about why this method can work for you.

I've tried all my networking contacts. Nothing seems to be working. I would like to do a strategic mailing campaign, but I don't have enough energy, and I don't know how to do a mail merge.

I can understand how you feel. The last month before I found my new job, I was fed up with the whole process. I can help you. I have a database of companies you can use. And I know from working with you that you are a quick study in software programs. I'll lend you my Word tutorial.

*Negative Stereotype: Over-40 workers resist change.*

## Why Should You Conduct a Strategic Mailing and Calling Campaign?

Does just the thought of networking send you into a panic? Are most of your opportunities halfway across the United States? You may be a prime candidate for conducting a strategic mailing and calling campaign. Take a look at some major reasons for launching your own campaign:

- A strategic mailing campaign can be less intimidating than networking. You can do it by e-mail, by regular mail, and through telephone follow-up.
- Your time commitment is less significant that it is for in-person networking.
- You can conduct the initial part of your campaign without leaving your home and without dressing for success.
- A properly conducted mailing and calling campaign makes you seem "sales savvy."
- You are tapping into the unadvertised job market as in networking.
- Less experienced workers do not usually bother to do this because it involves strategic planning.
- If you are a mature worker with mid- to senior-level experience, you will stand out from the crowd.

## How Do You Conduct a Strategic Mailing and Calling Campaign?

Richard was a savvy career-transition client who decided to leave no stone unturned. He extensively networked, searched the Internet, and conducted a strategic mailing and calling campaign. Following are the steps Dick took in his strategic mailing and calling campaign:

### Step 1: Create a targeted business list.

Use the Internet or the library to create a targeted business mailing list. Compile this list by industry, city, and state or county. If your list is too long, you can further define it by number of company employees. Your search may reveal your contact person, the hiring manager (such as the director of finance or the vice president of sales and marketing); or you may have to go to the company Web site or make a telephone call to obtain this information. If you are in outplacement or working with a career counselor, your may have access to online databases such as Dun and Bradstreet or Hoover's. If you don't have access, try these alternatives:

- www.corporateinformation.com covers businesses worldwide and is free. You can pull up companies by state and industry and then select them individually. You can obtain more than enough information for a targeted business list: the contact person, address, phone number, and so on. Because you cannot automatically create an overall list and must select individual companies, this is slow going, but you can obtain information on about 25 companies within an hour.

- www.datapartnersinc.com is the Dun and Bradstreet database. It is not free, but you can call 1-800-437-5446 for a price quote for an overall industry list that is customized and assembled for you. You can obtain contact information, addresses, phone numbers, and so on and have it sorted the way you want it.

- www.hoovers.com is a subscription-only database that provides the same information as Dun and Bradstreet and even more, depending on the level you purchase. You can contact Hoover's at 1-866-281-5974 for pricing information.

- www.forbes.com is a database of the top U.S. companies ranked by their financials. You can print a list by industry and state, but then you will need to locate other contact information on individual Web sites. This information is free.

I recommend that you create a list that will keep you occupied for a month. According to Richard, he could send out letters and call back about 40 contacts a week, so his original list contained 160 companies. (Most people are not this aggressive.)

I recently ran a search for a client, John, in the advertising industry in Chicago, and came up with a list of 87 companies, contacts, addresses, phone numbers, Web sites, and so on. I recommended to John that he stagger his mailing by sending out 25 to 30 letters per week and calling them the following week, at the rate of 5 per day. Accounting for mailing, calling, and follow-up, John will be working with this project for a month.

### Step 2: Verify your contact information before creating your letters.

Even if you buy business lists, you cannot be assured that the executive you planned to contact is still in place. Always look on the company Web site or call to verify the appropriate contact. As we all know, executives change companies frequently. Check out these two tips for getting more information:

- Ask for an executive profile when you call to verify contact information. This will give you customized information to include in your letter and help in your interview.

- Look for current news stories in your database or on the company Web site for additional custom information to use in your letter and in the interview.

### Step 3: Create an attention-getting letter.

The most influential book I have read about marketing to executives is *Selling to Vito* (Anthony Parinello, Adams Media Corporation). *Selling to Vito* addresses how to sell yourself and services to a *very important top officer*. My clients and I have successfully used the principles in this book to attract interest and achieve our call objectives. These are the key principles I have adopted from the book:

- Begin your letter with a statement in bold italics about yourself. It could be your own comment about yourself or a strong testimonial about you from a former employer. An example would be, "'Scott Dumas consistently exceeds annual sales goals in all economic conditions, and he is an exemplary motivator for the sales troops.' —Lucas Solard, Sr. Vice President, Motion Industries."

- Use the contact person's first name in your greeting. For example, use "Dear Patricia" instead of "Dear Ms. Jones." This may seem overly bold to those of you who were taught never to go on a first-name basis until you asked for permission. But, quite frankly, the "asking for first-name permission rule of business address is passé" unless you are recently out of college, in your 20s, or addressing a political figure or someone who is always called by their title. By getting on a first-name basis in your letter, you project higher self-esteem and establish yourself on equal footing with the person you are writing. I can say with great assurance that this method is effective in business correspondence.

- Include benefits to the employer in the body of the letter. Use easy-to-read bullets. If I were an administrative assistant, I might say that my strengths include the ability to be immediately productive in a fast-paced environment; recognized for tact and diplomacy under fire; highly skilled in Word, Excel, Peachtree Accounting, and PowerPoint; consistent team builder; and team player.

- Mention when you will call back in the closing sentence of your letter. For example, use "I will call back on Thursday, May 21st at 10:00 a.m. to discuss the possibility of meeting with you in person at a mutually convenient time." It is important to suggest the exact date and time for the potential telephone appointment. Of course, the addressee may be unavailable at the suggested appointment time, but your letter and callback show the seriousness of your approach. The reception to this approach was so favorable that one of my clients actually had an administrative assistant call her to reschedule the telephone appointment.

Following is an example of a letter using the *Selling to Vito* approach.

Always direct your letter to the highest available hiring manager. For example, after researching the company, an accountant might direct her correspondence to the chief financial officer or controller.

Remember that the object of your cover letter is to positively attract interest so that your follow-up call receives a positive response. The positive response can be an interview; learning that this business is not hiring now, but will be in six months; finding out you are not qualified for the position; or getting a lead to another company. A negative response is that your phone calls are never returned, which does occasionally happen.

*"Susan is the most outstanding supervisor I have ever worked with. She has consistently exceeded our expectations in customer service and cost savings."*

*—Don Jones, Vice President of Marketing, AAA Life*

Dear Richard,

Thank you very much for your time and consideration.

After more than 10 years of successful experience in life insurance and variable annuity administration, I am seeking a supervisory position in customer relations where I can contribute my strengths in

- Customer conflict resolution and retention
- Significant cost savings through attention to detail
- In-depth knowledge in life insurance and variable annuities

As you can see from the attached resume, my record is one of increasing responsibility. I am interested in exploring with you how my background might benefit your organization.

I will telephone you next Thursday, December 5, at 10:00 A.M. to discuss opportunities within your organization.

Sincerely,

Susan Kote-Tawia

*An example "Selling to Vito" letter.*

## Step 4: Send out a week's mailing with staggered call-back dates.

Richard sent out 40 letters a week and was able to call that many people back. He did not include the date and time on his letter, but he did indicate he would call back early the next week. His approach was good in that he did not rely on them to call him back. An even stronger approach is to state the date and time you will call them back.

When I first started my business, I sent out a staggered mailing to 100 corporations. I found that I could call only 25 a week. I blocked off specific days and times in my calendar to call back and left other time free to be out of my home. What happens after the first week is that call activity begins to mushroom. Like Richard, I found my success rate to be 10 percent in terms of interest, and at least 50 percent in terms of actual business from the 10 percent of interested companies. Richard found his success rate to be 10 percent in terms of a combination of interest and interviews.

In *Getting the Job You Really Want: A Step-by-Step Guide* (JIST Publishing), Michael Farr indicates that the average job seeker takes 24 interviews to land a job in an average time of three months, depending on the unemployment rate. (Recently the average reemployment rate has been five months, and longer for key executives.)

To get 24 interviews, he recommends spending at least 25 hours a week in the job search and setting a goal of one to two interviews a week. He says it requires 10 to 15 phone calls to get one interview. With so many initial interviews conducted on the phone, this is a realistic goal. The bottom line is that your interview success rate will be 10 to 15 percent—and probably 10 percent if you use the "Selling to Vito" cover letter from earlier in this chapter.

## Step 5: Call your contacts back at the designated time and don't give up.

When Richard and I began calling back, we frequently got voice mail or an administrative assistant. Following are the tips we share:

- **If you get the assistant, ask for the executive by their first name.** You will frequently be put through.

- **Explain to the assistant the purpose of your call.** For example, "This is Richard Cohen. I mailed John my resume last week and would like to speak to him briefly if I may." If the assistant screens you, establish a telephone appointment with the executive and build rapport with the assistant.

- **When you get voice mail, leave a brief message.** "This is Susan Kote-Tawia. I mailed you my resume last week. I am calling to establish a convenient time to speak to you on the telephone to discuss opportunities within your company. Please call me back at 878-504-3299. I will be available all afternoon and tomorrow morning before noon."

- **Don't give up.** Follow up, but don't over-do it. If you don't get a return call, try calling on different days and at different hours. One of my career applicants secured an interview and landed a new career after leaving eight voice mails spaced out over two months. She finally got her contact on the ninth call.

- **It is a good idea to intersperse voice mail with other types of contact such as a postcard, article of interest, and so on.** Statistically, an individual needs to hear about you five different times in order to make a buying decision, which begins with an interview. Varying your method of contact encourages your rate of success and keeps you from being a pest.

- **Reward yourself for making your calls on time.** I have always rewarded myself with a lunch, ice cream, or an exercise outing after I have finished my calls.

- **Reward yourself whether you reach your executive contact in person or reach voice mail.** Reward your consistency. The results of your efforts will pay off!

## Strategic Mailing and Calling Do's and Don'ts

| Do | Don't |
|---|---|
| Mail to the top hiring manager. | Mail to no name, wrong name, or HR Director unless requested to do so. |
| Include an exciting heading. | Send a ho-hum letter. |
| Describe benefits for the employer. | Be self-serving. |
| Call back as indicated in the letter. | Send so many letters that you know you cannot possibly make all the calls. |

| | |
|---|---|
| Use your networking script when you call back. | Be unprepared when you call back or expect them to call you. |
| Stay optimistic. It's a matter of numbers, time, and attitude. | Give up. |

## Effective Online Searches

Career consultants often undervalue online career searches. We see many career-transition clients whose idea of career search is limited to posting their resume on dozens of online job boards such as Monster and HotJobs. Five reasons that this online method is generally ineffective are

- Hundreds of resumes come to the same employer for one position. According to *Smart Money*, Monster received 24.5 million resumes in 2003 as compared to 1 million in 1999.
- The job postings are not always updated or removed.
- 70 to 75 percent of job opportunities are not listed.
- Many executive jobs and certain industry jobs are never listed online.
- Internet postings can result in spam and unsolicited calls from recruiters.

However, searching on the Internet can be an effective tool if you know which Web sites to use and how to use them.

I heard Jerry speak at a networking event about his online success and scheduled an interview with him. Jerry, age 48, landed a position as a software engineer with a major newspaper in slightly over four months, thanks to his Internet savvy and his strong interpersonal skills. He also received an increase over his former salary as a software engineer for a national bank. I wanted to know firsthand why he was staying in software engineering and how he conducted his Internet research. He had a potential age issue, and his reason for leaving the bank was that his position migrated overseas.

Jerry told me that he was staying in a volatile field because he felt that organizations would always have quality and coordination issues that would need to be addressed locally and not overseas. He felt that in a few years, he would be even more valuable because increasing problems would surface with overseas IT employment.

## Why Should You Conduct an Online Search?

After talking with Jerry about the results of his online search for employment, I am convinced that working online is a useful tool for every job search for company and position, and salary research; for posting resumes at selected portals and company Web sites; and for communicating with hiring managers and other contacts where e-mail is appropriate. (E-mail is appropriate in IT and telecommunication contacts, networking, and responding to openings when requested in this fashion. But never underestimate the power of a beautiful letter and resume on high-quality stationery.)

Although networking is usually credited with being the most effective job search method, I am seeing opposite indications from companies that are reporting that their major hiring comes through their own Web sites. So an effectively conducted Internet job search is certainly worth the time and effort.

## How Should You Conduct an Online Search?

Jerry's experience proves that a resourceful person can conduct a successful job search campaign by thoughtful use of the Internet. I found the following how-to tips to be true about online job searches:

- **Consider using a job search portal.** Jerry located www.worktree.com, which charges a very reasonable fee—$47 for three months, $67 for one year—to post your resume on industry Web sites, government Web sites, major job boards, overseas job boards, and so on. It's like one-stop shopping and has turned out to be quite effective. The site also has e-books available to members. You can also access recruiters at the site.

- **Keep your resume updated online.** Another tip Jerry gave me was, "After you've posted your resume, resubmit it at least twice a month so that your resume goes to the top of the list."

- **Make sure that you have a *Wow!* ageless resume and a dynamic cover letter.** If there is a job that you covet, follow up your Internet posting with a hard-copy cover letter and resume addressed to the hiring manager. Jerry said that he found his job through the job search portal. The hiring manager reports that what he remembers is receiving Jerry's beautiful hard-copy cover letter and resume.

  Jerry reports that he used a special cover letter format, called a "T letter," which compared how his qualifications met and exceeded the company's requirements. Chapter 4 presents an example of a T letter.

The bottom line is that you can find and attract an employer by sending your resume through a job portal, or through their own Web site, but what will sell the employer is your self-presentation, which includes your written resume and cover letter and how well you interview.

Even when you are conducting an online search, you must develop your interpersonal skills. When I heard Jerry speak to our networking group, I thought, "No wonder this guy found a job so quickly. He has an excellent sense of humor, good timing. He is a great storyteller and could be a stand-up comedian." (I know of what I speak, because I do corporate presentations with a stand-up comedian.) When you hear Jerry and are with him, you feel that he would fit in culturally with most organizations and would be enjoyable to work with. He certainly overcomes the negative stereotype that mature workers are a cultural misfit.

## Do's and Don'ts of an Internet Job Search

| Do | Don't |
| --- | --- |
| Be selective in your Internet posting. | Spend all your time in front of a computer screen. |
| Repost your resume every two weeks. | Leave your resume up forever without reposting. |
| Follow your Internet posting with a hard copy of your resume and cover letter. | Rely only on your Internet written presentation. |
| Apply on company Web sites and selected portals. | Plaster your resume on all job boards and include your Social Security number on your resume. |
| Use current keywords and submission requirements. | Disregard keywords in your resume and submission requirements. |
| Determine whether your position and industry are suited to an Internet job search. | Rely on the Internet as your only job search method. |

## Answering Ads in the Newspaper

Never underestimate the power of a local newspaper, such as the *Atlanta Journal and Constitution,* or a national newspaper, such as the *Wall Street Journal,* for locating a job. Although this may seem to be a low-tech approach, it has a higher success rate than large Internet job boards—some sources say as high as 12 percent. And many newspapers also post these ads on their own Web sites. Newspaper ads are usually for entry-level to medium-range positions, with the exception of the *Wall Street Journal,* which posts senior- and executive-level positions.

Here are some do's and don'ts for answering newspaper ads.

### Do's and Don'ts for Answering Newspaper Ads

| Do | Don't |
|---|---|
| Apply for the job if it is a close match. | Apply for the job if the match is questionable. |
| Answer the ad late in the first week to avoid the the crowds. | Answer the ad on Monday with the rest of the world. |
| | Respond to the ad the way that you choose instead of the requested way. |

## Partnering with Others in Your Job Search

Ten years ago, personnel agencies, retained search firms, and executive recruiters were a "no-sweat" way to manage your job search without having to network heavily, do strategic mailing and calling, or spend time looking at ads.

Personnel agencies, retained search firms, and executive recruiters remain excellent resources, but because of the growth of the Internet, many companies are no longer employing them or are employing them less in order to save money. Companies are relying instead on their own internal recruiters and Web sites to attract candidates. (The exception is in the search for key executive positions such as Chief Operating Officer, where executive recruiters and retained search firms are frequently employed.)

Your personal situation determines whether you should research and contact personnel agencies, retained search firms, and recruiters. Read on to find why and when, as well as the do's and don'ts of working with job search firms and individuals.

Before we proceed, I want to give you this caveat: Beware of scams. I have recently had two clients who paid between $2,500 and $6,000 up front to a business that claimed to guarantee job results. These clients received inferior resumes, outdated business lists, and mass mailings of their resume with an ineffective cover letter. My clients diligently followed up on their resume mailings with no positive results and were desperate when they came to see me. You've heard the adage, "If something appears too good to be true, it probably is." This applies to the job search assistance business.

## What Do You Need to Know About Using a Personnel Agency?

Of all the groups you can hire to help you find a job, contingency personnel agencies have the most job listings, and the employer pays them a fee only if they fill the position. There is no charge to you. Keep the following three points in mind as you consider using a personnel agency:

- Use contingency agencies if you have an easily classified position, such as staff accountant, administrative assistant, or insurance claims adjuster.

- You can locate contingency agencies in the *Yellow Pages* or online under personnel agencies in your city. Also, most states have an association of personnel consultants. Georgia's, for example, is the Georgia Association of Personnel Consultants (GAPS).

- Choose contingency agencies that specialize in your position and your industry.

## What Do You Need to Know About Using a Retained Search Firm?

Retained search firms charge a company a fee or retainer to fill specific positions for a defined period of time. Again, there is no fee involved for you. A retained search firm usually conducts its own search of currently employed candidates and does not actively encourage job seekers to contact it. Some companies do allow you to post your resume on their Web sites. You may get lucky and catch their attention. Be aware of the following points when considering using a retained search firm:

- Use a retained search firm when it approaches you. Treat your interview with the firm seriously.

- If you are highly compensated and have impeccable experience in a senior corporate management position, approach retained search firms through their Web sites or a networking contact.

- You can find a database of retained search firms at www.kennedyinfo.com. The three largest are Korn/Ferry International, Heidrick and Struggles Inc., and SpencerStuart.

- If you have a career specialty in a certain industry, such as Webmaster in IT, use a specialized retained search firm, such as Matrix Resources (www.matrixresources.com).

## What Do You Need to Know About Using an Executive Recruiter?

The executive recruiter is usually more interested in finding you than having you contact him or her. However, if the recruiter has strong contacts with major firms and your current position is in demand, he or she may be willing to champion your cause. Following are a few tips for working with an executive recruiter:

- Definitely use executive recruiters if they approach you. Treat interviews with them seriously.

- If you have impeccable experience in senior management or a high-demand position, you can approach executive recruiters through their Web sites or through networking.

- To find an executive recruiter, search on the Internet by using the keyword *executive recruiter* and your city in a search engine such as Google.

- If you have difficulty finding an executive recruiter, you may need to buy a list. You can buy a master list of executive recruiters tailored to your position, industry, and location for $1 per recruiter with a $30 minimum at www.kennedyinfo.com.

## Do's and Don'ts of Hiring Others to Conduct Your Job Search

| Type of Service | Do Approach If You | Don't Approach If You |
|---|---|---|
| Contingency agency | Have an easily classified position that is in demand and a solid track record of consistency and achievement. | Are making a dramatic career change, have a difficult-to-classify position, spotty work history, or low achievement history. |
| Retained search firm | Are a highly compensated, marketable senior executive with a solid, consistent track record of achievement. | Are entry- to mid-level, not highly compensated, and are not marketable because of your position, industry, inconsistent work history, or poor track record of achievement. |
| Executive recruiter | Are well compensated and marketable, mid- to senior level, with a solid, consistent track record of achievement. | Are not well compensated and marketable, or entry level, without a solid, consistent track record of achievement. |
| Temporary and contract employment agencies | Look for agencies that specialize in your position or industry. These jobs are a great filler and a good way to find a new job. | Expect to make your normal salary or get perfect assignments. |

## Organizing Your Search

Whether you use one or multiple job search methods, organizing your efforts is critical. In no time, you will have applied for multiple positions over the Internet, through newspaper ads, in mailing campaigns, and so on, and the calls will start coming in. If you are not organized, one day you will get a phone call from an HR professional or hiring manager and have no recall of the company, the hiring manager, or the position. This very bad feeling is one that you want to avoid.

You can easily organize your job search using an alphabetized accordion folder and filing information by company. I personally prefer the accordion folder to an index-card box because the folder will hold your letters, ads, postings, company research, and so on. Keep this folder by your telephone. You can establish a callback diary by using an ACT software program, an Excel spreadsheet, or a simple filing system of employers to call on Monday through Friday. This could be a card index system; or even easier, keep one folder open in your accordion system for next-day calls.

A helpful hint for staying on track is to set daily networking, calling, and mailing goals. Preparing these goals and pulling supporting information the afternoon or night before you call allows you to sleep soundly, feel refreshed, and get started early the next morning. A bonus is that the right side of your brain processes these contacts overnight and helps you be more creative.

## Choosing Your Strategic Search Methods— Online and Off

No two career candidates are alike, and their search methods should not be alike, either. Here's what I mean:

- One of my 52-year-old senior retail management clients found her position through networking. She never searched online, used a retained search firm, or did a strategic mailing and calling. She instinctively knew that networking was the way to go for her position in the retail industry.

- On the other hand, a 48-year-old software engineer found his position online but also networked on the side. He hedged his bets by using two job search methods that were both appropriate for his position and his industry.

- And then there's the 57-year-old telecommunications sales manager who networked, posted his resume online, worked with executive recruiters, and then landed an outstanding position by a strategic e-mail campaign to key executives. He used all methods appropriately and simultaneously.

There is no one-size-fits-all approach to job searching. Choose the approaches that best fit your position, industry, personality, and age. As a rule, networking is an excellent approach for mature candidates. Strategic mailing and calling also works. The Internet can be productive if your position is among those frequently posted. The newspaper can be effective for frequently posted and unusual, seasonal, and part-time positions. Retained search firms and executive recruiters love highly compensated senior managers but will often hesitate to represent anyone 60 or older.

And remember that there is always the "strange attractor" or the unique way that you can present yourself that works for you and hasn't even been discovered. One of my clients discovered his last position on the bulletin board of his church. This was the only place the position was posted.

The more employers hear about you in multiple ways, such as getting a letter, getting a phone call, hearing about you from a referral, and so on, and the more types of search methods you employ, the greater the chances that you will be successfully employed.

---

### What Job Search Methods Will You Use?

Take a moment to select the job search methods that you are willing to explore and then make a few notes on how you plan to approach each opportunity.

- Networking

_____

_____

- Strategic mailing or calling

_____

_____

- Online searching

_____

_____

*(continued)*

---

*(continued)*

- Searching in the newspaper

_____

_____

- Partnering with others

_____

_____

# CHAPTER 7

## Achieve Memorable First Impressions
### Avoid the Most Common Interview and Networking Mistakes

*"What you are speaks so loudly, I can't hear what you say."*

—*Ralph Waldo Emerson*

At 9:30 A.M. I was reviewing Raphael's resume for the second time before our ten o'clock interview. His resume was a knockout, and I was anxious to meet him in person. Several puzzling questions floated around in my head about him, however. The first was this: "Would a former corporate regional manager and a Major in the U.S. Army overpower me and the entire office?" And, second, although I could not tell his age from his resume, "Would he have the energy and patience for this stressful job?"

Raphael was dressed in a well-fitting navy blue suit, a starched blue oxford-cloth shirt, and a coordinating geometric-print tie. His salt-and-pepper hair was thick and curly. He walked energetically to meet me, looked me straight in the eye, shook my hand firmly and warmly, and said, "Gail, it's a pleasure to meet you. Thank you so much for taking the time to meet with me today." His voice was clear, pleasant, and not overly loud. And I thought to myself, "So far, so good. Let's see what this man has to offer."

In this chapter, you'll find out how to create a dynamic personal advertisement composed of attractive visual and vocal components that will result in a second interview, a referral, or a job offer.

## The Importance of the First 60 Seconds

First impressions are formed within the first 60 seconds of meeting someone and are made up primarily of visual cues and vocal energy. Visual cues account for 55 percent of what people believe; vocal energy accounts for 38 percent; and information, only 7 percent (according to Right Management Consultants, based on the studies of Albert Mehrabian).

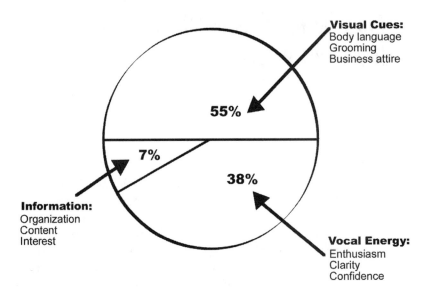

*The cues people use to form first impressions.*

Because a memorable, standout first impression is created in an extremely short period of time, it's critical for you to send positive visual and vocal cues that say, "I'm friendly, self-confident, intelligent, energetic, and people savvy." I have never met a serious career-transition client who wanted to deliberately send a message that says, "I'm unfriendly, have low self-esteem, have low physical and mental energy, and am not interpersonally sensitive." Those negative visual and vocal messages are usually sent because job seekers are unaware of how they are being perceived by their interviewer or networking partner.

Although it's true that first impressions can be strengthened or corrected during the interview or networking conversation, it's hard to overcome a strong negative first impression. If you want people to believe the best about you, you must show them before you tell them.

## Recognize That You Are the Product: Your Presence Is the Advertisement

Do you know that you are your product, and the first impression that you create is your ad? Thirteen years ago, my husband and I sold a 35-year-old home (we were the second owners) with an enticing ad that read

> Charming Cape Cod home totally renovated with designer kitchen and Jacuzzi bath; well-landscaped lot on $^3/_4$-acre cul-de-sac.

Before the house underwent an inexpensive renovation, a "deadly" honest ad would have read

> Thirty-five-year-old Cape Cod home for sale. 20-year-old avocado green appliances in the kitchen still work well and compliment chipped linoleum floor and counters. Toilet leaks infrequently. Good fixer-upper.

Which ad do you think would attract more buyers and most effectively support the price we wanted for our home?

Writing the enticing ad for our home led us to the conclusion that we needed to renovate it. We inexpensively updated the kitchen appliances by professionally spraying them white (without getting too much paint on the dog). We added new flooring, refaced the kitchen cabinets, and replaced the countertops. We enlarged the bathroom, replaced the old tub with a Jacuzzi (that we didn't get to enjoy), and installed a new bathroom counter. The house was completely updated and the yard was well landscaped. Our renovated home was consistent with our new ad.

When it came time to show our home, we played to a potential buyer's five senses: The house was a visual knockout; soft classical music was playing in the background; an apple pie was baking in the oven; fresh macadamia-nut cookies were placed on the counter; and fabrics, rugs, and lighting gave the house a luxurious feel. We were thrilled but not surprised when our home sold quickly for top dollar.

*Before a pre-interview*          *After.*
*makeover.*

Makeovers and photos courtesy of Peggy Parks (peggy@theparksimagegroup.com).

If we had posted the enticing ad, which correlates to you writing the best resume and cover letter possible, but left the house "as-is," what a difference! Potential buyers viewing the home would have discovered that their on-site impression was not consistent with our written ad. The house would not have sold for top dollar or would have been on the market longer, or we might be still living in it.

When you write the best *Wow!* ageless resume possible and consistently create and present a positive interview and networking personal appearance, you too will sell yourself more quickly for top dollar. On the other hand, if you elect to present yourself "as-is," and "as-is" looks outdated, frumpy, slumpy, and unenergetic, you will be perceived as old and unattractive. Your product, You Inc., will not sell on the market quickly for top dollar.

In the next few sections, I will share with you the key elements that positively affect an interview and networking first impression. In order to create a vivid, positively memorable impression, you as a career client, like a home seller, must also appeal to the senses by offering an image that looks good, sounds good, smells good, and feels good. Fortunately, you don't have to be concerned about tasting good.

## The Key Elements That Positively Affect First Impressions

The key elements that positively affect interview and networking first impressions are these:

- Erect posture and confident, energetic body movements
- A dynamic, enthusiastic, clearly understood voice
- A clean and properly groomed appearance
- Appropriate and stylish business attire
- A relaxed, centered composure

Let's take a look at each element and find out how it relates to your sensual impression and how you can use it to your advantage.

### Use Erect Posture and Confident, Energetic Body Movements

When a career candidate vigorously walks into my office with head held high, smiles sincerely with full eye contact, and firmly shakes my hand, I am favorably impressed. Wouldn't you be? A vigorous walk with head held high signals energy and self-confidence.

On the other side of the coin, a tentative walk with poor posture signals low energy and insecurity, and makes me think of Frasier's dad on the sitcom. When you walk energetically with head held high, you are definitely counteracting a potential negative stereotype associated with some older workers, which is that older workers have low energy and may not have the stamina to do the job.

A candidate who makes full eye contact, smiles, and firmly shakes my hand without squeezing so hard that my ring cuts into my fingers gets my vote for being confident, energetic, and friendly. That candidate is demonstrating optimism and a positive attitude, recognized as two of the three most important hiring criteria. (The three characteristics that employers seek in their selection process are optimism, a positive attitude, and aptitude.)

In many ways, your 60-second first impression is an informal test that reveals your optimism or pessimism and a positive or negative attitude. Optimism and a positive attitude are physically revealed in the first 60 seconds of a first impression whether in person or over the telephone.

*"Over 50 companies now use optimistic questionnaires in their selection process to identify people who have not just talent and drive but also the optimism needed for success."*

—Learned Optimism, *Martin Seligman*

The combination of smiling, firmly shaking hands, and walking into an office with energy and erect posture is a win-win approach for you that will make a favorable first impression on your interviewer or networking partner. You can elevate their mood *and* your mood, and improve your own position, by using such approach.

In the first impression you make, you will have positively influenced the interviewer's visual sense through your smile and erect posture and energetic body movements. And, as a bonus, with your firm, warm handshake, you will have positively appealed to his or her sense of touch.

## To Make a Positive First Impression

- Stand and walk erectly with your head held high.
- Walk vigorously.
- Smile sincerely and give direct eye contact.
- Shake hands firmly.
- Warm cold hands with hot water or a hand warmer. (In the winter, I place HotHands hand warmers, available in discount department stores, in my pocket or gloves. I store the HotHands in the glove compartment of my car.)

- Practice your nonverbal presentation with family and friends; get their feedback.
- Visualize yourself as mature runway model.

## Project Vocal Energy and Enthusiasm

When Tanya walked into my office and enthusiastically greeted me with a firm, warm handshake and then said in a moderately loud, clearly, and energetically paced voice, "Gail, I'm Tanya Baker. I've been looking forward to meeting you," I immediately recognized that Tanya was confident, energetic, friendly, and articulate. If she had walked into my office and sat down in a chair without greeting me, or tentatively peeked in my door, or greeted me with a low voice using garbled, hesitant speech, I probably would have concluded that she was lacking in self-confidence and energy, was unfriendly, and was not articulate.

Concentrate on raising the volume of your voice and pace of your speech in order to create a winning vocal first impression. Speak a little louder and faster than usual and clearly articulate your words. My caveat or warning (excuse the former attorney in me) is don't overdo the vocal energy and enthusiasm; don't speak so loudly or talk so fast that you bowl over an interviewer, or you'll create a negative first impression of someone who is inconsiderate, aggressive, and cocky.

Recently, I had a candidate who bowled me over with his voice. He was a 6-foot-4 former basketball player with a booming, almost gruff voice. As his career consultant, I encouraged him to "soften" his voice, which, combined with his forceful appearance, was intimidating. I was afraid that he would overwhelm a potential employer.

### To Project Positive Vocal Energy

- Speak in a moderately loud voice without overwhelming.
- Speak with an energetic pace.
- Clearly articulate your words.
- Smile and speak with enthusiasm.
- Practice with family and friends and get their feedback.
- Tape your greeting and get feedback on your voice.

## Polish Your Telephone Voice

Have you ever guessed what a person looked like based on their voice, making assumptions about age, energy, intelligence, and self-confidence? Be honest.

In your career search, your initial 60-second first impression often occurs over the telephone, where vocal tone and energy account for 93 percent of the impression. Interview screenings, networking opportunities, information-gathering calls, and appointment setting are all conducted over the telephone. These phone calls are usually your second opportunity to create a positive first impression after an employer has received your *Wow!* ageless resume and cover letter. So make every effort to reinforce and strengthen your positive first impression with a standout telephone voice.

This means that you must be careful to speak in an upbeat, self-confident voice when you place or answer a call. How can you find out how you sound? Practice sending and receiving prospective interview-related calls with a friend who will be honest with you. (An interview-related call is a follow-up call to a prospective employer after you mail a cover letter and resume, or a call to a net-working source to determine the potential for employment with their company.) Get feedback on your friend's impression of how you sound. Your friend should evaluate your vocal delivery and the content of your message. Do you speak in a clear, sincere, warm, and energetic voice? Do you sound prepared, but not over-rehearsed? Is your message clear and organized? Are you a good listener?

Another good way to get vocal feedback is to call your own telephone number and leave yourself a 60-second commercial or *elevator speech.* Critique yourself and then have a friend critique you.

### To Create a 60-Second Practice Commercial

- Call a friend or your own voice mail.
- Give a greeting and then ask how the person is doing.
- State your name.
- Share your reason for leaving your last employer or changing careers.
- State the reason for your call.
- Ask for honest feedback.

Can a caller determine your age by your voice? I don't think so unless you sound tired by projecting a soft, slow voice. I can usually judge the age of a young woman because of a higher voice; our voices usually lower with age, but I usually can't guess age unless someone is over 70.

## Speak Professionally When You Answer the Phone

I've had two bizarre telephone turnoffs involving telephone calls to career candidates. One time, a gruff-sounding spouse answered the phone with a growl. I didn't want to call that number again! And then there was the time I called and received a voice mail with scary Halloween music. Can you imagine a potential employer's first impression of you being created through a gruff spouse or a scary ghoul?

If you're busy or stressed when the phone rings (maybe you're cooking or heading out the door), let the call go into your voice mail so that you can return the call when you're upbeat and prepared to talk to the caller. Never sacrifice the quality of your telephone calls to 24/7 accessibility.

Also, encourage spouses, significant others, and children not to answer your primary contact phone when you're in the job search process. If you want to be totally safe and can afford it, get your own dedicated telephone line while you are searching for a job.

Recently, I interviewed Susan Boone, a therapist, about her positive telephone conversation. I asked, "How do you always project calmness over the telephone?" Susan said that she makes a point not to answer the phone on the way out of the door or when she is distracted. Letting her calls go into voice mail allows her time to "get her thoughts together." Susan makes it a point to project an emotional feeling of enthusiasm and calmness in her voice.

## Prepare a Formal Voice-Mail Message

On more than one occasion, I have been shocked by a career candidate's voice-mail message (or lack of one). Having a professional voice-mail message is important, but not difficult. It should be a simple but dignified message, such as "This is Ron Swanson. I'm out at the moment, but if you'll leave your name and phone number and a brief message, I'll get back with you shortly."

If you leave your cell phone number on your voice-mail message or are using your cell phone exclusively, remember to be upbeat and professional when you answer the cell phone.

If you don't have voice mail, you probably are missing out on potential employer calls. When I call a candidate and there is no voice-mail service on the phone, I conclude that this person is not taking his or her job search seriously. It's not terribly expensive: You can get voice mail from your phone carrier for approximately $5 a month or buy an answering machine for approximately $50.

Caller ID is another telephone feature you might want to explore. It is a real help in knowing when to spontaneously answer the phone and when to let the call go into voice mail.

According to Norman King, author of *The First Five Minutes* (Prentice Hall Press), a lower-pitched voice is associated with self-confidence and integrity. A higher-pitched voice is associated with fear and nervousness. This applies to your voice in person, over the phone, and on your voice mail. Recent surveys have also revealed that we associate faster speech with greater intelligence.

Your pleasant, enthusiastic voice appeals to an interviewer's sense of hearing. If the interview is over the phone, you can also create a positive visual and emotional image with your voice.

## To Create a Winning Vocal First Impression over the Telephone

- Be prepared for the call.
- Speak enthusiastically with increased vocal volume and pace.
- Practice your 60-second commercial with a friend or through your own voice mail.
- Slightly lower your voice if needed.
- If you are unprepared to receive a call, let it go into voice mail.
- Never sacrifice quality of vocal presentation for accessibility.

### Reduce Your Regional or International Accent for Clearer Communication

A regional or international accent can be entertaining and lucrative, if you're given an opportunity to use it as a career. Have you ever heard Dixie Carter, from the '80s TV series *Designing Women*, use her Southern drawl to promote BellSouth Yellow Page advertising? How successful would the *I Love Lucy* TV series have been without Desi's Hispanic accent and his famous line, "Lucy, you've got some 'splainin' to do!"

Regional and international accents can be charming and don't have to be completely eliminated unless your voice is difficult to understand, grating or nasal, or you mispronounce and misuse words. If you "murder the king's English," so to speak, or have a totally unpleasant vocal tone and are hard to understand, your intelligence and professional competence will be discounted.

Although a first impression contains very few words, you will feel more confident in all interviewing and networking situations if you know that you are clearly understood. One of the best ways to "correct" a regional or foreign accent is to record a short narrative or poem and have a trained speaking professional or voice therapist critique your performance and personally work with you.

Some of my clients have chosen to record the "Fire and Ice" poem by Robert Frost because of its brevity and humor. The poem also contains a number of words that are frequently mispronounced such as "fire" and "twice." You can find the text of this poem online at www.bartleby.com/155/2.html. Try reading it out loud.

You can pick up your pace and learn to enunciate correctly by reading a limerick quickly and pronouncing each word clearly. Two short limericks to try are these:

> How many chucks would a woodchuck chuck if a woodchuck could chuck wood?

> and

> If Peter Piper picked a peck of pickled peppers, how many pickled peppers did Peter Piper pick?

One of my clients, a human resources manager, shared that a new accounting recruiter actually mispronounced the word *resume* by making it rhyme with *costume*. Can you imagine someone saying, "Please let me see your resume (re-zoom rather that re-zuh-may)?" It would certainly give you less than a positive impression.

Speaking clearly is a critical part of creating positive interview and networking first impressions. Although your initial impression time is short (60 seconds), make the most of it. Clearly speaking in person and over the telephone will dramatically enhance your vocal presence and positively influence every interview or networking opportunity.

## Improve Your Personal Hygiene and Grooming

The senses of smell and sight are positively and negatively affected by personal hygiene and grooming. All of us, at one time or another, have experienced bad breath, body odor, dandruff on our collar, or some other grooming mistake. These olfactory and visual signs are turnoffs to a hiring manager. Usually, we're not even aware that we have these personal hygiene issues. Often a significant other or friend will not tell us for fear of offending. We've seen dandruff and smelled bad breath and body odor on others, but we usually can't see it or smell it on ourselves.

Bad breath is frequently the result of the beginning of gum disease, often a problem as we get older. Other signs of gum disease are sensitive and bleeding gums. Coffee breath and cigarette breath are easier to cure. Don't drink coffee immediately before an interview, and don't smoke a cigarette, which can affect your breath and your clothes. Beware of eating garlic the night before an interview. A good breath check involves licking your tongue on your hand, letting the moisture dry, and smelling your hand. Also there are two quick ways to improve your breath: drink water or eat an apple.

Check for body odor in your clothes and shoes. Make sure everything you wear is clean. Choose a deodorant that won't fail under interview pressure and networking stress. Antiperspirants work best during stressful times.

Dandruff is easy to cure with an over-the-counter shampoo containing coal tar. Notice your jacket when you take it off. Does it reveal dandruff? Take a look at your glasses. Are they dirty or do they have dandruff on them?

On rare occasions, I have seen a candidate with extremely wind-blown hair or a slip hanging below her skirt. Those problems can be prevented if you arrive early for an interview or networking meeting in time for a last-minute mirror check.

Nails should be clean and well shaped. Clothes should be clean and expertly pressed. Pay attention to all of the small grooming details that give you a "bandbox" look.

As a second-time single woman 20-plus years ago, I wanted to look my personal best and attended Barbizon School of Modeling for a nine-month course. My primary intention was not to become a professional model, but to learn the subtle nuances that would transform me from a slightly frumpy teacher to a dynamic, marketable single woman. Although I learned fantastic posture and runway modeling, the most useful information for me came in the form of dressing and conversational tips. For instance, most women I know try to match their shoes to the color of their skirt or pants. A more attractive, coordinated look involves matching shoes and stockings, for example, camel suede pumps with stockings close to the same color. Accessories definitely "punch up" clothing for men and women, such as a man's colorful tie or a woman's scarf. However, you have to be careful not to overdo accessories. For example, wearing rings on many fingers and multiple earrings is considered bad taste. Also, the quality of clothing, shoes, and leather accessories is critical.

I learned that you don't have to be wealthy to be well-dressed. At Barbizon, many of the professional models shopped at designer resale shops, and I have adopted this practice for myself.

The good news is that I landed a wonderful corporate job soon after my graduation from modeling and law school. I learned from the interviewer's comments to me after I was hired that my initial first impression was definitely enhanced by my clothing, grooming, and confident presence. Landing a husband took a little bit longer. I was single eight more years.

I learned in class today that I need a new interview outfit, including up-to-date shoes, and that I should consider dyeing my gray hair. I'm really feeling reluctant not to present my real self!

You can be attractive and real at the same time. Updating your image is not so difficult. A new suit and shoes would increase your interview self-confidence, and I have a good hairdresser I can recommend.

*Negative Stereotype: Older workers are fearful.*

## Choose Appropriate and Stylish Business Dress

Twenty-eight years ago, John Molloy in *Dress for Success* recognized and capitalized on his version of how the *upwardly mobile executive* should look. Our definition of professional business attire still owes much to his early influence. John Molloy's upwardly mobile executive look later became known as the "IBM look" and consisted of male and female versions of dark suits, white shirts, and subtly striped or patterned ties or scarves. Today we jokingly refer to people who take this look to extremes as "suits."

*A client before a pre-interview makeover.*

*After.*

Makeovers and photos courtesy of Peggy Parks (peggy@theparksimagegroup.com).

You may be so used to business-casual dress at work that you may not have a formal business suit in your closet. You may wonder, "What's the fuss over dressing for the interview when the interviewer will be in business casual?" The fuss over dressing for the interview in a suit involves an interview tradition that is centuries old, like the handshake, but was perfected by John Molloy in the late seventies. Unfortunately, interviewers still expect to see candidates wearing a current version of the "dress for success" look.

If you don't own a stylish, well-fitting business suit and are on a tight budget, you have several reasonable options, which I have used myself. You can shop for a well-fitting suit or dark sport coat at an upscale resale shop, buy a suit or sport coat on sale, or borrow a suit or sport coat from a friend.

You announce your serious commitment to the job by wearing appropriate and stylish professional business dress for your interview. You can dress appropriately and stylishly on a very limited budget. Read on to find out about color choices and appropriate accessories.

## Choose Business Dress with Flair

Despite the fact that the interviewer may be dressed in business casual, you need to wear the male and female equivalents of a conservative well-tailored suit in blue, black pinstripe, brown, gray, or camel (women only), but now you can add a colored shirt, shell, or blouse. Men can choose a white or shade of blue shirt and a colorfully patterned tie.

Women can wear a blouse or shell of almost any color except orange. Women can wear a skirted suit, but a pantsuit works better for mature clients unless they have great legs and are willing to wear stylish but potentially uncomfortable heels. Stockings are always required for an interview, despite the sandaled, no stockings, painted-toe look that is now popular in warm weather.

Shoes and portfolios should be conservative and of high-quality leather in basic colors. Jewelry and makeup should be minimal but in good taste, with a watch and pen of high quality. Strong perfume and cologne are a turnoff.

You can add energy and warmth or coolness and sophistication to a business-professional look by using color appropriately. A woman's red blouse and a gray suit can be warm and energizing. A man's blue pinstriped shirt with a blue suit can project coolness and sophistication.

*Before.*                    *After.*

Makeovers and photos courtesy of Peggy Parks (peggy@theparksimagegroup.com).

## Makeover Examples

When John walked into my office for a video mock interview, he was wearing a gray suit, white shirt, and gray tie. He had gray hair and wore brown and black Hush Puppies. What impression did he create from his appearance? He looked gray and comfortable. I read him as conservative and not particularly fashion conscious. My first impression based on his clothing alone was neutral, not negative, but also not positive. His suit and pressed shirt told me that he was

*Before.*          *After.*

Makeovers and photos courtesy of Peggy Parks (peggy@theparksimagegroup.com).

making an effort to promote himself, but the dull, gray tie and Hush Puppies said that he was outdated in his wardrobe, and suggested that he might be outdated in other areas. I immediately began to try to "punch up his appearance" to project more energy and currency. I gave him this prescription for a simple makeover:

> "Leave your hair gray. Wear your gray suit with a colorful tie that coordinates with your suit. The gray suit will look wonderful with a medium-blue shirt. Leave those Hush Puppies at home."

When I first met Inga, she presented an entirely different first impression in her attire. She wore a pinstriped black pantsuit with a royal-blue blouse and stylish black-leather pumps. Inga carried a black-leather portfolio. Her hair was stylish; her jewelry was minimal; her watch was gold with a black strap. Her nails appeared to be professionally done, and her makeup was tasteful. Although I knew that she was over 45, there was nothing old or dated about her appearance. She looked "with it," energetic, and totally professional. At the end of the interview, I complimented her on her positive first impression. I gave her this prescription:

You go, girl!

## Choose Your Interview and Networking Wardrobe Carefully

When in doubt about your networking and interview wardrobes, just turn to these suggestions, using those that appeal to you or meet your needs:

- Talk to a well-dressed career consultant or an image consultant.
- Observe and present a mature version of a professionally dressed 35- to 45-year-old.
- Look at well-dressed professionals in fashion magazines such as *InStyle* for women and *GQ* for men.
- Consult with your children if they are fashion conscious and knowledgeable.
- If you have definite figure flaws such as waistline bulge or a double chin, get advice on how to use clothing and makeup to minimize these issues.
- Visit a savvy sales professional in a high-end clothing store for advice.

Many of these wardrobe suggestions won't cost you more than your time. You can go to a bookstore and study recent fashion magazines, or seek the advice of a savvy sales professional, even if you do not plan to buy your suit until a later date.

Most importantly, seek out honest advice, not just what you want to hear. Also, make sure that the person giving you the advice is well-groomed and fashion conscious. And, don't ever wear clothing that is too tight or too large.

*Before.*          *After.*

Makeovers and photos courtesy of Peggy Parks (peggy@theparksimagegroup.com).

You have to be especially vigilant during your career campaign to look your professional best at all times, because you never know when a casual encounter will turn into a job interview. One of my savvy career clients wears makeup on the StairMaster at her athletic club because of the extensive networking opportunities she recognizes in every environment. After all, you never know whom you'll run into at the gym, grocery store, or library.

### Know When to Wear Business-Casual Attire

Is it ever appropriate for you to wear business-casual attire? Business-casual attire is sometimes appropriate for networking and interviewing *if* business-casual is the "accepted company attire." In some interview sessions, it may be appropriate to wear a blazer and slacks with a turtleneck or open-collared shirt in place of a suit. Company insiders are the best people to advise you whether their company is one of the few in which business-casual dress would be appropriate for an interview.

However, it's smarter to be overdressed in terms of formality for a job interview or networking meeting than to be underdressed in terms of business casual. Recently, recruiters have indicated that candidates frequently wear sloppy business-casual dress to interviews and are in serious need of a professional image consultant.

### Handle Gray Hair with Care

My clients are always asking me about whether to dye their gray hair. Gray hair is associated with old age, but we all know that some of us look more distinguished with gray hair than others. And some of us are prematurely gray in our 30s. If you look like the well-known actors James Brolin, also the husband of Barbra Streisand, or Richard Gere, your gray hair is an asset because you are famous and have a young-looking face. If you don't look like Brolin or Gere or the female equivalent, you will not be committing a sin by coloring or frosting your hair.

Before coloring your hair, it's a good idea to get the opinion of your career consultant, your hairdresser, or an image consultant. You might ask whether you should color your hair, and if so, what shade would look best. Also, you might seek advice on the attractiveness of your haircut. Have your hair professionally colored unless you are already a pro at this.

Recently one of my career clients asked about dyeing his mustache. He was balding and didn't have to worry about his hair. I told him to go ahead and dye his mustache, using the special hair color available today for mustaches and sideburns that partially covers gray and yet still gives a natural appearance. Why not? What did he have to lose? The next day all the women and men in his career-transition workshop applauded him because his dyed mustache made him look more vigorous.

## Trim Those Beards

Neatly trimmed beards are acceptable if you can't stand to part with them, but the Santa Claus look is out unless you want to be hired at the mall for Christmas. If you keep a neatly trimmed beard, it may not be an impediment to landing a job, but be aware that many organizations still harbor distaste for beards. Some people feel that a heavily bearded look is not open and friendly. Beards are more acceptable in education and artistic positions, such a professor, architect, media consultant, and so on.

## Beware of Very Long Hair and Teased or Overset "Mall Cuts"

Longer than shoulder-length hair on women over 45 presents an outdated look. Longer than shoulder-length hair is generally not considered business professional for the younger generation, and on older women the outdated look is magnified. A fresh haircut or putting long hair in a stylish updo works well. Having outdated, unprofessional hair can reinforce a negative stereotype that you are a cultural misfit within the organization. Extremely long hair fit in at Woodstock but is passé in today's business environment.

I once had a talented but snobby hairdresser who referred to highly curled, sprayed, perfectly coiffed hair as "mall cuts." The message that he was sending to me was that contemporary hair should not look perfectly cut, sprayed, and set, but should look natural and a little wind tousled.

## Male Hairstyles Matter, Too

Men should wear their hair stylishly short without a ponytail unless they are applying for an artistic endeavor. Too-short hair tends to look like the male equivalent of a "mall cut," so it's a good idea for you to get a haircut the week before, not the week of, an important interview or networking meeting. Also, try to avoid an obvious comb-over to cover a balding head.

### Professional Hair for Business

- Professional hair for women is stylishly cut and no longer than shoulder length.
- Longer hair can be put in a stylish updo.
- Professional hair for men is short and stylishly cut.
- Coloring gray hair, sideburns, beards, and mustaches often presents a more youthful appearance.

## Avoid the Danger of Presenting Yourself "As-Is"

At this point, you may be thinking, "Oh, Gail, I just don't want to or can't color or restyle my hair or buy a new business suit. I want to present myself 'as-is'." I commiserate with you because I've had the same feeling myself. Most Saturday mornings I sleep in, go without makeup, and put on a baseball cap to hide my messy hair. Jeans and a sweatshirt complete my rumpled Saturday look. But I know that in any professional work environment I need to look my professional best, or I lose my credibility as an author, career consultant, and professional speaker.

When you are thinking this way, remember that you can use subtle temporary hair color; have a friend put your hair up, and buy your business suit at a resale shop. You can inexpensively look your best.

If you are strongly resistant to changing your personal image, I recommend that you ask yourself these questions:

- Are you shooting yourself in the foot and eliminating many potential career opportunities by being a nonconformist in small things?
- Why are you opposed to a more youthful look?
- Are you just being stubborn and lazy?
- What if you love your new look?

Yes, a few employers will take you "as-is," but you may not command top dollar.

## Minimize Self-Expressive, Sexy, or Ethnic Dress

In a class I teach on interview techniques, a very articulate corporate trainer expressed her desire to wear African-American dress to networking and interview events. My answer was to suggest that she wear traditional professional business dress with a tribal patterned scarf or self-expressive ethnic pin.

When my clients ask me about wearing self-expressive dress, I can empathize with them. My personal wardrobe consists of a lot of funky and semi-sexy clothes: fur sweaters, flashy rhinestone earrings, and tight black jeans (with Lycra, of course). My personal research, mistakes, and experience confirm that my corporate and career clients will not find me credible as an author, career consultant, and professional speaker if I present a business image that is a combination of a skinny version of Miss Piggy and Dolly Parton.

However, I can express myself appropriately by wearing a brown tweed business suit, an azalea pink shell, and a flashy pin of many colored stones.

When you're considering self-expressive dress, ask yourself these questions:

- Is your dress appropriate and stylish attire for your prospective business environment?

- Are you dressing appropriately for the organizational role that you want to play in the future?

- Are you recognizing and honoring the perception of the interviewer?

Interviewers tend to hire someone who seems like themselves and who appears to fit in culturally within the organization. If your dress doesn't match, you'll be better off to modify it to reflect suitable business attire for that cultural environment.

A few environments seem to tolerate extreme self-expression: artistic environments and behind the scenes in technology and telecommunications, but never in the interview process itself. If personal self-expression is worth that much to you, perhaps self-employment or the entrepreneurial route is your cup of tea.

## Face the Fear of Change

Changing your appearance and your dress can be uncomfortable, but personal growth and improvement occurs by embracing change. Remember that action precedes feeling. Who's to say that you will not enjoy having brown rather than gray hair, or won't fall in love with your new pinstriped suit or your resale blazer?

Can you financially benefit by lowering your voice or buying a new interview suit? Small first-impression changes can definitely energize your career search, and image consultants claim that changes in appearance and the impression you make can add 20 percent to your salary.

Wild animals don't need image consultants; they naturally assume the coloration of their environment in order to prey on instead of being preyed upon. By assuming the professional colorations of your future business environment, you will fit in colorfully and culturally; and you'll not only survive, but potentially receive a higher salary offer.

---

### Appropriate and Stylish Business Dress

- Business suits in blue, brown, black pinstripe, and camel (women only) are always appropriate.
- Colored shirts, blouses, and ties project energy, authority, and sophistication.
- High-quality leather shoes and portfolios are a must-have.
- Minimal jewelry and tasteful makeup are appropriate.
- Hair, beards, and mustaches all benefit by being stylishly cut and even touched up with hair color.
- Use business-appropriate and stylish self-expression in your dress.
- Seek help from the professionals: hairstylists, career-transition consultants, image consultants, and clothing sales professionals.

---

All first impressions rely heavily on visual and nonverbal cues, which include posture, body language, voice, smell, and touch. Giving such heavy emphasis to first impressions may seem shallow, but it's of critical importance in your career search. Making a few small personal changes can cause you to be employed more quickly and command a higher salary. Believe me, a makeover is worth it!

---

### To Create a Winning First Impression

- ❏ Are you displaying erect posture and walking vigorously?
- ❏ Are you projecting vocal energy and clarity on the phone and in person?
- ❏ Are there details of personal hygiene that you need to address?
- ❏ Is your business appearance appropriate and stylish?
- ❏ What do you need to change to create a no-holds-barred positive first impression?

---

*"Interviewers aren't necessarily looking to hire clones of themselves and their colleagues, but they do usually want to hire people who have a similar air about them."*

—*Michelle Tullier,* The Unofficial Guide to Finding a Job

## Dealing with Anxiety, Stress, and Those Ole Interview Blues

The job search process is a time when those of you who are normally high strung and full of energy may become "strung out" to the point of exhibiting physical signs of extreme anxiety. You may perspire more than normal, talk too fast, shake, speak in an unreasonably high voice, and so on. When I conduct video mock interviews, I see all these signs of interview stress and anxiety. I also see career candidates licking their lips, swallowing, coughing, pulling their hair, playing with their clothes, and gesturing overdramatically.

Even if you are not anxiety prone, you may feel blue and temporarily depressed about having to continue putting yourself out there. You may begin to mentally sing those "Poor Me" and "Why Me?" career-transition blues and may want to withdraw from social contact.

Feeling blue or temporarily depressed usually shows in your demeanor. You may appear sad, slump, speak too softly to be heard, and have difficulty remembering names and events and clarifying your thoughts. Sometimes you may even lose your sense of humor. When I conduct a video mock interview, I can read depression in body posture, lack of smiling, a furrowed brow, a limp handshake, and a tentative greeting.

I have personally felt and exhibited many of these same anxiety and "singing the blues" –driven behaviors before, during, and directly after an interview, networking event, or corporate presentation. These feelings are natural in the career-transition process, but it's important for you to learn to manage them and change them to present a positive first impression. The following sections share some of the techniques I use to calm myself when I am anxious or energize myself when I am feeling blue.

### Manage Your Mood Before You Leave for an Interview

In many ways, going to an interview or a special networking event is like professionally speaking or acting. Here's what you can do to prepare for any interview:

- Prepare and lay out your clothes and accessories the day before your meeting.

- Assemble your props: portfolio, coat, umbrella, purse, and so on.

- Always bring extra resumes and business cards.

- Practice the interview questions we will cover in Chapter 8, "Ace Tough Interview Questions."

- Research the interviewing company and your interviewer.

- Practice the correct pronunciation of the interviewer's name.

- While you're still at your computer, use Yahoo! or MapQuest to print a map to the interview site.

- Plan to arrive at your destination at least 30 minutes early, and use some of the extra time to take a restroom break to check out your hair.

- Remember that traffic and confusing directions can easily take up to 30 extra minutes, so build extra time into your traveling plans.

- Take your cell phone and the company telephone number in case of an emergency.

## Practice Positive Self-Talk

Toot your own horn before the interview. Tell yourself how wonderful you are. Remember and self-vocalize past career and interview successes. Say, "I am calm, prepared, and relaxed," and you will be. Remember that action and thought precede feeling. "Relax" is an action verb.

## Exercise and Roar in the Car

One of the best ways I've found to control my anxiety is to exercise before an interview or presentation. If I have time, I take a brisk walk in the neighborhood to get my positive endorphins going.

In the car on the way to the interview or presentation, I open my mouth widely and scream, pant, roar, and laugh (but I don't do this if my convertible top is down). This stress-relieving technique is known as "The Lion's Roar."

## Indulge in Small Pleasures

If I have time before an interview, I stop to enjoy a breakfast or lunch of my favorite comfort foods, which range from a cheese omelet with harvest grain and nut pancakes to a new favorite, a smoothie with yogurt, peanut butter, and banana.

## Reward Yourself Regardless of the Outcome of the Interview

In a previous highly successful international sales career, I learned to always reward myself daily for making all my sales calls, even if I didn't score an appointment or sale. Building in a reward after the interview will cause you to look forward to your meeting. The reward could be joining a friend for a movie, dinner out, or a visit to a bookstore to buy a new bestseller. Choose whatever you personally find rewarding.

### Visualize a Positive First Impression

Imagine yourself happy, relaxed, and smiling as you greet your interviewer. Notice that your breathing is regular. Imagine the pleased expression on the face of your prospective employer. Picture the positive interview outcome you desire. Remember that some interviewers are uncomfortable and inexperienced and your pleasant, stress-less demeanor will help them relax. Interviewing is always a two-way street. They are interviewing you, and you are interviewing them.

### Seek Inner Stillness

I always allow myself a few moments before I go "on stage" to pray, meditate, or read scripture. Pausing and breathing deeply will provide a mini-mental retreat and refreshment for you.

### Count Your Blessings

Think about all the things you feel happy about before you go into an interview or networking situation. Your face will reflect your happiness.

I know that you may not have time to try all these stress and anti-blues techniques before a single interview, but choose the ones that appeal the most to you. My message to you is to do what it takes to project a positive aura that makes others want to spend more time with you.

## Put It All Together

Like it or not, you are judged in the first 60 seconds of any meeting, so give it your best shot. Plan to stand out in the crowd. Create a visual, vocal, and total sensory presence that will make everyone in the room look at you admiringly when you enter. Watch for consistency in all aspects of your written, visual, and vocal presentation. Recruiters strongly declare that personal appearance and self-confidence are key factors in closing our own personal sale, landing a job.

The balance of power has shifted when you are asked to interview. Before the interview, the interviewer, recruiter, or employer holds about 75 percent of the power. When you are invited to interview, the power shifts more in your favor. This fact alone can increase your self-confidence.

When you designed your *Wow!* ageless resume, using the guidelines in Chapter 5, you were careful to create an ad that would present a desirable image of energy, talent, experience, and so on. The first impression you make in an interview is your on-site advertisement, so take care in creating a memorable first impression.

## What Kind of First Impression Do You Want to Make?

Describe your ideal first-impression image.

What do you look like?

_____

_____

What are you wearing?

_____

_____

What do you sound like?

_____

_____

How do you feel?

_____

_____

What are you willing or able to change about the following so that you can create your ideal first-impression image?

Personal appearance:

_____

_____

Interview wardrobe:

_____

_____

Voice:

_____

_____

Hygiene:

_____

_____

Mood:

_____

_____

# CHAPTER 8

## Ace Tough Interview Questions
### Avoid Discrimination and Negotiate Your Best Offer

*"Concentration comes out of a combination of confidence and hunger."*

—*Arnold Palmer (1929)*

"When the recruiter interviewed me over the telephone and asked me, 'How many years of experience do you have in pharmaceutical sales?' I answered '22 years.' I could tell by the abrupt way he shortened the call that he was discriminating against me because of my age. How do you think I should have handled the call, and do you think he was really discriminating against me because of my age?"

Jackie posed tough questions for me. These were my answers to her. "Jackie, the first thing we all want to do is to get through the preliminary screening process involving our resume by showing no more than 10 to 15 years of relevant work experience. So a good answer to the recruiter's question about your years of experience in the pharmaceutical industry might have been 10 or 15 years, or 'How many years of experience are you looking for?' followed by a confirmation that you have this level of experience. I think that the recruiter shortened the call because he had marching orders from the employer for a person with less experience. This was not age discrimination per se, but it was discrimination because of perceived overqualification for the job."

This chapter can help you overcome your interview anxiety by covering tough and age-related interview questions. It will also show you how to negotiate your best salary and benefits offer.

## Avoiding the Three Most Common Interview Pitfalls

The three most common pitfalls that you may face in the interview process are these:

- Failing to effectively address age-related and discriminatory questions
- Ad-libbing tough interview questions
- Accepting a job offer on the spot without negotiating your best compensation

Whether you have recently been in the job search process or haven't searched for a job in years and are feeling rusty, your age and experience can make you unrealistically overconfident or unrealistically underconfident. Throughout your life and career, you probably have had the chance to hone your communication skills and feel comfortable with a wide range of people in a variety of situations. Having these experiences and skills and the confidence that comes along with them is wonderful and will certainly come in handy in interviews, but believing that you can spontaneously answer interview questions—particularly those that overtly or covertly deal with the age issue—is a big mistake. Conversely, if you haven't interviewed in years and are worried about the issue of your age and lack of recent interview or related work experience, you may fail to present your "best self" in the interview process.

This chapter provides you with a variety of successful answers and tactics for these sensitive areas. Let's start with the age-related, potentially discriminatory questions.

## Understanding Why Employers Ask Age-Related Interview Questions

Employers and recruiters are generally better prepared in the interview process than they were in the past because of the wealth of formal how-to-interview information at their disposal. My husband and I have conducted many seminars on successful interview techniques for employers. There are many books on interview techniques, so employers and recruiters have hundreds of formal interview questions already written for them.

If you are interested in seeing things from the interviewer's perspective, you may want to review 96 *Great Interview Questions to Ask Before You Hire* (AMACOM). The author, Paul Falcone, presents a variety of behavioral interview questions (questions about how you have acted in a past or hypothetical situation that can serve as a predictor of how you will act in the future). He tells interviewers how to interpret a candidate's answers, and points out red flags in the interview process.

Employers ask age-related and potentially discriminatory questions for a number of reasons:

- Simple curiosity to determine your exact age
- A desire to determine whether you live up to age-related negative stereotypes such as using the job as a bridge to retirement or being a cultural misfit (not fitting in the organization)
- Out of ignorance and insensitivity in terms of age discrimination
- A desire to find out why someone with your level of experience would apply for this job

Chapter 5 talks about how to create a *Wow!* ageless resume that emphasizes your strengths and deemphasizes your age. This chapter covers what to do after that resume gets you in the door. In the next section, you take a look at positive answers to age-related interview questions that will emphasize your strengths and deemphasize your age. You'll see a variety of different examples, but there's one caveat: Use these suggested responses as a springboard for developing interview answers that sound natural—no, that *are* natural—because they are in your own words. Practice composing answers to all of the interview questions you can find, not just those that relate to age.

## Acing the Five Key Age-Related, Potentially Discriminatory Interview Questions

There are hundreds of interview questions that a potential employer can ask. From all these questions, I've selected five that have the greatest potential for you to display your strengths and defuse age-discrimination issues. I've also shared positive ways to frame your answers. Because an interviewer might ask all of these interview questions either directly or as a part of a hidden agenda, it's critical that you listen with all your senses—including your intuition—and effectively answer even the implied questions behind what the interviewer is saying.

Chapter 2 discussed the negative stereotypes that some potential employers hold about older workers. Here are some of the most common stereotypes that you might encounter:

- You might use the job as a retirement bridge, not giving it your full attention or future concern.
- Your salary requirements might be too expensive, and it would be a waste of time to interview you.
- You might not fit in with a younger boss, coworkers, or clients.
- You might not have the mental and physical energy or stamina to be a peak performer in the position.
- You might not be happy, or might be bossy, because you are overqualified for the job.

Fortunately, not all prospective employers hold negative stereotypes about older workers. However, there are enough out there who do that it pays to be aware of their issues and anticipate their questions. The following five age-related interview questions are directly connected to the negative stereotypes mentioned earlier. Remember that these questions will usually not be asked verbatim, so be on the lookout for them to be disguised in subtler wording. The five questions are these:

- Will you be using this job as a bridge to retirement?
- Are you too expensive?
- Will you be a cultural misfit when working with younger bosses, coworkers, and clients?
- Do you have enough energy, stamina, and brain power to do the job?
- Are you overqualified for this job?

## "Will You Be Using This Job as a Bridge to Retirement?"

I was thrilled to receive a letter from Marie, a recent participant in my "Age as an Advantage in Your Career Search" class. This class explores how to present the strengths you bring to the employment market, as well as how to overcome the negative stereotypes employers associate with age. Marie had spent 20 years as an administrative assistant after being "CEO" of her household. She was not exactly thrilled about reentering the job market at 60. When she came to our career-transition services, she had no resume and had never formally interviewed. She feared age discrimination and wanted to be as prepared as possible for all aspects of her job search. At a "job-landing party" and in a letter to us, Marie described how she overcame the "job as a bridge to retirement" issue.

In Marie's own words:

> Finally, I pulled together all my interview knowledge from my career-transition services and went off to the interview with butterflies in my stomach. I thought, "They will laugh at this 'old lady' applying for this wonderful job." I gave it my best shot and decided to use a suggestion that Gail had used in her "Age as an Advantage" class. When the hiring manager told me that the job was open because his administrative assistant had decided to retire and play in the yard, I used that as my opportunity to address my own retirement. I told him that I was such a people person and enjoyed the business world so much that retirement was not in my vocabulary. I could never see myself staying at home and playing in my yard. I said, "Being part of a team is what makes me the happiest."

I just got a call from Judy. Marie's waiting for you in the lobby. I peeked around the corner. She's got a lot of gray hair. She's probably easing into retirement!

Well, you could be wrong. She has great credentials and got here early. She may be as energetic and open to challenges as the best of us.

*Negative Stereotype: Older workers use their jobs as bridges to retirement.*

Marie landed this key administrative assistant position in a high-tech company on her first interview. She was pleased with her compensation, and her commute is now under 15 minutes. What Marie did right in her interview was to openly and positively address the unspoken question voiced by the hiring manager, "Will you use this job as a retirement bridge?" Her answer was an emphatic "No!"

Frequently, the retirement bridge question is disguised as "Where do you expect to be five years from now?" or "What are your long-term career goals?" Because this question may not always be asked, it is helpful if you address it openly as an answer to a comment as in Marie's case, or in the frequently asked first interview question, "Tell me about yourself."

Marie's resume is in Chapter 5, "Create a *Wow!* Ageless Resume." Her resume contains such focus and energy, as well as a strong record of accomplishments, that I am not surprised it got her in the door. But it was Marie's savvy interview answers that got her the job.

Should you address the retirement bridge question if it has not been formally or informally asked? Whether you should proactively address the retirement bridge issue is a judgment call based on your individual circumstances. My rule of thumb is that if you are over 50, look your age, and are applying for a traditional corporate position other than senior management, it is to your benefit to openly address the "bridge to retirement" issue. On the other hand, if you are at the younger end of the spectrum of mature workers and are youthful looking, don't bring it up. Or, if you are applying for a job in an obviously age-diverse industry, the subject may not be an issue.

Several months ago, I conducted a video mock interview with John, a former sales manager in the food industry, who appeared to be in his early 50s. As I looked over his resume, he volunteered enthusiastically, "I may seem to be a bit far down the road in my career in terms of experience, but I am excited about this opportunity and have the energy and drive to make a positive contribution to your company." He made a believer out of me. He preempted any questions I might have had about his retirement and reassured me of his energy and drive to be a future sales manager. If I had been conducting a real interview, I would have hired him.

> ### To Address the "Job as a Retirement Bridge" Question
>
> - Decide in advance whether your personal situation warrants proactively bringing it up.
> - Prepare and rehearse your comments to this question prior to the interview.
> - Be prepared to answer this question when asked directly, indirectly, or through the interviewer's comments.

The two examples—Marie and John—positively illustrate how to turn around a potentially damaging, but not illegal, age-related interview question. It is critical for you to know which questions are illegal, why they are asked, and your options for answering them. We discuss EEOC (Equal Employment Opportunity Commission) recognized illegal interview questions later in this chapter.

## "Are You Too Expensive" and "Will You Be a Cultural Misfit?"

The best way to see how these questions and answers play out is for you to read actual interview examples provided by my clients. Guy, a former vice president in charge of new business sales for a major telecommunications company, was a participant in my "Age as an Advantage" class. When I brought up the negative stereotype that most employers believe that older workers are too expensive, Guy shared this with the group:

> I've been in the job market for a year. I've been asked frequently what I made on my last job, and what my salary expectations are for the new job, but I've never shared what I made on my past job or my salary expectations for the new job. I'd like your opinion on whether my answers are hurting me.

When I asked Guy what he normally said when asked about his past salary in a telephone or in-person interview, his answer was that he said he would be happy to discuss salary when an offer was put on the table. He boldly resisted all attempts by the interviewer to arrive at his past salary or expected salary. In the past year, he had a number of interviews, but he had never received a job offer.

Guy is an imposing person, a former college basketball player who is tall and muscular, with a full head of black hair and a dominant and charismatic personality style. His voice is deep, almost gruff. I immediately suspected that his answers to the salary question were at the root of his problem. I asked him to role-play the salary question with me in front of the group. He was happy to accept my challenge. Here's the context of our interview related to the salary issue:

**Gail:** "Guy, what were you making when you left Swedish Telecom?"

**Guy:** "I will be happy to discuss salary when the position is offered."

**Gail:** "I need to know what your salary expectations are in order to determine whether you are in our ballpark and to decide whether we can take you to our next level of interviews."

**Guy:** "I believe we can work something out if you feel that my qualifications are suitable for the position."

**Gail:** "Guy, you've got some good answers here, but I still need to know what your salary expectations are for this position."

**Guy:** "What is your salary range for this position?"

At this point in our interview session, I was getting hot under the collar. I was ready to jump across the table and shake Guy, and I am not known as a woman who is hot tempered. The class was sitting on the edge of their seats, waiting to see what would happen next. I let Guy know in no uncertain terms that he was irritating me, and that if I had been a potential employer, I would have ruled him out of the selection process because he was displaying stubbornness and inflexibility, and was not appreciating the need to answer the question of salary from the interviewer's perspective.

From our role-play, I recognized that Guy was unconsciously reinforcing two negative stereotypes associated with age. By not revealing his past or future salary expectations, he was implying that he might be too expensive. He was also indirectly suggesting that he would be a cultural misfit—stubborn, inflexible, and unyielding. When I asked Guy why he didn't suggest a salary range for the new position, he said that he was concerned that his previous triple-digit-plus income would under- or overprice him because telecommunications currently had a variance of at least $100,000 in the salary range for a senior sales management position. Guy had also been encouraged by outplacement classes and interview books that he should not reveal his salary in the early interview stage. The problem was that Guy was taking these suggestions too literally.

I minced no words with Guy. Here was my prescription:

> Guy, if you're getting the interviews, you're doing a great job of marketing yourself. Where you're going wrong in the interview process is in your answers to the salary question. When asked about salary, be prepared to give a salary range that you have researched and then get the interviewer's feedback. If there is such a variance in the position you are applying for, choose a midrange. You can hedge once, but not more than once.

Guy became one of my private clients, took my suggestion, and began to reveal his expected salary range in interviews. Within two weeks, he received, negotiated, and accepted a much-welcomed and acceptable job offer. He attributed much of his success to my remark that he should have "reasonable expectations in a tough job market." Guy limited his negotiations to one session, but he did receive a sign-on bonus and feels that, although his base salary is somewhat less than his last position, the new job affords greater possibilities for future promotions in terms of title, responsibilities, and salary.

I invited a well-known senior executive recruiter from Korn/Ferry International, a retained executive search firm, to the "Age as an Advantage" class the following month. He told us in no uncertain terms that if you are evasive about your salary with a recruiter, the recruiter will refuse to represent you with a future employer. The recruiter needs to know what he is working with, and past salary is always an indicator of future salary.

In a situation in which you are directly interviewing a screener or a hiring manager, you can tactfully deflect a direct answer about salary at least once. However, if you sense irritation or you are into a second or third interview, you need to provide a salary range that the interviewer can work with.

Here are some excellent ways to respond to salary questions. You can try these answers once without offending a recruiter. On the second go-around, try to give a salary range that you have researched.

**Question:** *(Asked during first personal interview.)* "Can you tell me about your salary and bonus arrangements at Alex and Alex?"

**Answer:** "Rather than make salary an issue at this point in the process, I would prefer to discuss salary in light of the opportunity presented and my potential contribution."

**Question:** *(Asked during a telephone interview.)* "What are your salary expectations for this job?"

**Answer:** "Due to the sensitive nature of this question, I would prefer to discuss salary in a personal meeting."

**Question:** "What did you make during your last year at Martin Technology?"

**Answer:** "I don't feel that the two jobs are comparable. Could you tell me more about the position with your company before we discuss salary?"

**Question:** *(Asked during second personal interview.)* "What are your salary requirements?"

**Answer:** "I've researched the salary range for this position in our area and have found a salary range from $125,000 to $175,000, plus bonus. Is this what you have in mind?"

Another good answer is, "I am at a point in my life where salary is not my only criterion. I will be happy to consider your offer if you feel that I am the right person for this position."

**Question:** *(Asked during third interview after hiring manager indicates a desire to have you as an employee.)* "What will it take to bring you on board?"

**Answer:** "I have researched this position and have found a salary range from $125,000 to $175,000 plus bonus. Is this what you have in mind?"

These answers show the interviewer that you are well prepared and articulate. The salary question is one of the most difficult interview questions to answer at any age. It is especially sticky when you are over 40, because you may be overpriced in today's market and also afraid that revealing salary will screen you out. Or, you may be changing careers and want to be evaluated on your transferable experience rather than being paid on the same basis as a younger worker fresh out of school.

```
┌──────────────────────────────────────────────────────┐
│        To Successfully Answer a Salary Question        │
├──────────────────────────────────────────────────────┤
```

- When presented with the salary question, first respond with a smooth, noncommittal answer.

- Remember that the interviewer is fishing. Don't begin salary negotiations until you receive an offer.

- If pressed to give your salary expectations, give a salary range based on your research.

- Keep your cool and make it to the next interview.

- Don't antagonize the interviewers; be sensitive to their feelings.

- Practice several smooth answers for different situations.

## "Do You Have Enough Energy, Stamina, or Brain Power to Do the Job?"

As you age, your energy may decline, and you may fail to project energy in the interview process. Chapters 2, 5, and 7 discuss specific ways to counteract the low-energy, negative stereotype with descriptive and colorful resume language and memorable interview first impressions, including energetic body language, strong vocal responses, and vibrant business attire.

It's unlikely that you will ever be asked whether you have enough energy and stamina to perform this job. Rather you may be asked some of the following questions:

"How do you feel about working in a fast-paced environment?"

"Are you able to come in early and leave late?"

or

"Describe a recent work experience where you were under extreme pressure with a tight deadline."

Also, the energy question may never come up, but may be an unspoken question when they see your gray hair or the extensive career experience on your resume. Here is a positive way to address the question about energy and stamina, even if it is not verbalized:

**Question:** "Are you able to come in early and work late?"

**Answer:** "I've always had a lot of energy and enthusiasm for my work, and I'll continue to do what it takes to produce a quality product and meet and exceed deadlines.

For example, when I worked for Broadband, I was asked to get out a last-minute request for proposal by noon the next day. At 5:30 P.M., I was the only one left in the office. I worked until 7 P.M., organizing my data, making a list of the remaining research material needed. I alerted my support team by telephone and e-mail to meet me an hour early the next morning. The first thing in the morning, I gathered my team together, assigned remaining research and production, and gave them an accelerated deadline. We produced an excellent proposal on time and were awarded a multimillion-dollar contract. I was proud of my team and proud to have directed the project."

Notice how the answer and the specific example reinforce the job candidate's energy and enthusiasm. Also, pay attention to the fact that the candidate was a team player, but also accepted credit for the direction of the project. The candidate used a specific technique called *STAR,* an acronym for Situation, Task, Action, and Result. This is how the technique was used in the interview situation and how you can use it to your future benefit:

**Situation:** Our sales department at Broadband had a last-minute request for proposal to respond to by noon the next day.

**Task:** I heard about the proposal as I was leaving the office at 5:30 P.M. and the rest of the crew had left for the day. It was my responsibility to make sure the proposal was completed by noon the next day.

**Action:** I worked until 7 P.M., organizing the data and making a list of the remaining research material needed. I alerted my support team by telephone and e-mail to meet me an hour early the next morning....

**Result:** We produced an excellent proposal on time and were awarded a multimillion-dollar contract. I was proud of my team and proud to have directed the project.

Using the STAR technique will cause you to give the specifics that interviewers love and remember. Be sure to choose an example with a positive result and accept credit where credit is due.

## To Find Clues About the Job During the Interview

The question about your energy level is one way that the interviewer gathers clues about how your age might affect your ability to handle the job; it also provides clues for you about the job itself. When the interviewer brings up direct or indirect questions about your energy and stamina, make a mental note to probe into the job demands, hours, deadlines, and overall expectations at an appropriate time.

## Using the STAR Technique

Take a moment now to practice the STAR technique by writing your answer to the following interview question related to physical energy, stamina, and brainpower.

**Question:** Tell me about a recent business experience when you were under intense pressure.

**Answer**

| Situation | Task | Action | Result |
|-----------|------|--------|--------|
|           |      |        |        |
|           |      |        |        |
|           |      |        |        |
|           |      |        |        |

Interviewers may also believe that our brains have slowed down. This impression is especially strong in the technology industry, where new systems, software, and processes are constantly being introduced. This may be an unspoken question when they see you in person or look at the years of experience on your resume. Their issues could be couched in a question such as "Tell me about a recent goal you have set." Or, "What have you been doing since you left Equite besides looking for a job?"

I suggest two effective ways of handling this question: using the STAR technique when asked the questions, and proactively bringing it up yourself when asked the question, "Tell me a little about yourself."

**Question:** "Tell me about a time when you recently multi-tasked."

**Answer:** "First of all, I am an expert in time management, and although I multitask very well, I have learned to group like activities and take them to a certain stage of conclusion before moving on. On Friday morning, I was working in my virtual office, handling my e-mail and other computer activities. I e-mailed our receptionist and discovered that I would be teaching 15 employees in the Monday-morning training program and 18 in the afternoon. I completed my computer work, which consisted of altering a PowerPoint presentation, and then checked my workshop handouts, making the necessary extra copies for Monday. I also made extras to spare for the session the following month and packed my briefcase for Monday.

"I check three business phone lines daily for messages, including my mobile phone. On Friday afternoon, my supervisor called me on my virtual office business line with an unexpected emergency/opportunity for me to cover, so I quickly jumped into my business clothes and headed out to a client meeting on the other side of town."

## "Aren't You Overqualified for This Position?"

The question of overqualification frequently comes up for mature career candidates, especially if you have listed 20 or more years of experience on your resume, which I generally do not recommend. (10 to 15 years of relevant experience is generally sufficient.) Behind the question of overqualification are many negative age-related stereotypes, which verbally would sound like "We probably cannot afford this candidate," or "She will be bored and move on to another company." Or, "He won't fit in (will be a cultural misfit) and will probably try to take over my job" (will have difficulty reporting to a younger boss). Your goal in answering the question of overqualification is to emphasize the strength of your experience, highlight your accomplishments, and counter these negative stereotypes.

Ruth was being interviewed for an internal human resources consultant's position with a major entertainment conglomerate. She had made all the right moves up to this point, networking her way into the interview, listing only 15 years of relevant experience on her resume, dressing stylishly for her interview, and consciously projecting energy. During the successful interview this question came up:

**Question:** "Why do you want to work for us? You appear to be overqualified. You were in a senior management position with Abbott, and you've had your own business for the past five years."

**Answer:** "I enjoyed my stint in management, and I'm looking forward to being a successful part of your consulting team. In fact, rather than thinking of myself as overqualified, I like to think that you'll actually get more bang for your buck!"

**Question:** "How do you feel about working for a younger boss and with younger team members?"

**Answer:** "At Abbott, I had the privilege of working with people of great age diversity. I reported to a CEO who was 10 years my junior, and I had one team member who was certainly my senior. I believe that my experience and wisdom will be a welcome addition to your team, and I'm looking forward to meeting them in person."

Ruth handled the overqualification question very well by emphasizing her strengths and flexibility, and made it to the next set of interviews, which involved all her future team members.

Sometimes the overqualification question is the salary question in disguise because a long career with great credentials usually equals a high salary. Another way to deal with the overqualification question is illustrated in the following example.

**Question:** "You seem a bit overqualified for this position."

**Answer:** "Can you help me understand your concern so that I might specifically address it?"

By asking a question of clarification, you will gain insight into how best to answer the question.

| To Deal with the Overqualification Question |
| --- |
| ■ As you answer the question, emphasize your strengths and accomplishments instead of your years of experience. |
| ■ The overqualification question may represent an unspoken issue of salary or cultural misfit. |
| ■ Probe to determine the unspoken question behind the question. |
| ■ The overqualification question may also represent an unspoken threat to the hiring manager. |
| ■ Stay positive and answer the issues behind the question. |
| ■ Feel free to use your sense of humor in answering the question. |

# Answering Illegal, Age-Related Questions

The Age Discrimination in Employment Act (ADEA) of 1978 prohibits employment discrimination against applicants aged 40 and over. The first area of job hiring in which we see subtle or blatant age discrimination is in the resume-screening process. This is why Chapter 5, "Create a *Wow!* Ageless Resume," recommends that generally you list no more than 10 to 15 years of relevant work experience, and include only recent educational dates.

The second area where subtle and blatant age discrimination occurs is in the interview process. Most interviewers are savvy enough not to ask you directly, "How old are you?" or "When were you born?" They attempt to find out your age indirectly by asking you questions such as, "When did you graduate from Walker High?" or "I have a friend who graduated from Duke. When were you there?"

Although there is disagreement among authorities about whether asking for a college graduation date is illegal, because people go to college at different ages, the questions about age and high school graduation dates are illegal. You don't have to answer them. However, it's been my professional experience that many employers ask these questions out of ignorance of the law and out of simple curiosity as to your age. Usually they are unaware that they are asking age-discrimination questions.

The way you answer these questions can make or break your interview. You have a number of choices:

- Graciously refuse to answer the question. "I really don't think it is appropriate for me to respond."
- Use your sense of humor. "I was at Duke in the '80s." (You were there for your class reunion.) Or "You know that a woman never tells her age!"
- Tell the truth. "I graduated from Walker High in 1961."
- Address the interviewer's unspoken question. "I am incredibly energetic and I expect to be working a long time."

My recommendation is that you answer questions about your age in a nonconfrontational manner that demonstrates that you are indeed a savvy communicator with a sense of humor and no chip on your shoulder.

---

### To Address the Illegal Age Question

- Graciously refuse to answer.
- Respond with humor.
- Answer the question behind the question.
- Keep the atmosphere positive.

---

Should you take legal action if you feel that you were discriminated against in the hiring process? Discrimination in the hiring process is difficult to prove, and you may be better served to move on to an age-diverse employer or other opportunity. However, you can seek the counsel of an EEOC representative who will determine whether you have a solid case. Then, take time to decide whether you are prepared to commit the necessary time, energy, and expense to the case.

---

### Preparing for Age-Related Questions

Being able to ace age-related interview questions is not an improvisational experience. These questions should be addressed proactively and practiced before your interviews begin. Take time in the space below to work out your answers to the following questions.

1. "When did you graduate from _____ _____ (postsecondary school)?"

_____

_____

*(continued)*

*(continued)*

2. The interviewer is asking you for the third time, "What are your salary expectations for this position?"

_____

_____

3. "This job will involve 50 percent travel." (The implied question is "Can you handle it?")

_____

_____

4. "What are your long-range goals?"

_____

_____

5. "How do you feel about reporting to a younger boss?"

_____

_____

## Preparing for Other Tough Interview Questions

Many other interview questions and conversational openings provide opportunities for you to emphasize your strengths and accomplishments and deemphasize age, such as "What are the accomplishments that you are most proud of?" and "Is there anything else I should know about you?" These questions give you an opportunity to describe situations and accomplishments that are in direct contrast to the negative, age-related stereotypes discussed in previous sections.

For example, Guy, previously mentioned in our "potentially too expensive" example, was asked, "When you work for us, what will you say to yourself when you get up in the morning?" Guy responded, "I look forward to coming into work and being part of a successful team, not being intimidating, but being a valuable resource." Guy's response showed that he was a great fit in a team-oriented sales environment and aided his later salary negotiations. Just as Guy did, you can look for opportunities to proactively address and counteract negative age-related stereotypes.

Many other interview questions are difficult, not because they are specifically discriminatory, but because they are too broad or vague to be easily answered. Following are some I have selected from those that have disturbed my job-seeking clients, as well as a few described by Michelle Tullier, author of *The Unofficial Guide to Finding a Job* (John Wiley & Sons). In her book, Michelle lists and describes 15 of the trickiest questions. She says this about them:

> "...you'll find questions that make you pause due to their wording, scope, or 'squirm factor.'"

The *squirm factor* means a question that causes us to discuss negative personal factors, controversial subjects, or personal failures. Let's face these tough interview questions together in the following worksheet.

---

### What Will You Say?

Read the question and possible responses. Then write an answer that you might give in the blank lines.

1. **"Tell me about yourself."**

   **A good answer:** "I am a high-energy, people-savvy guy. For the last five years, I have been human resources director for ABC Telecommunications. I am proud of recently revamping our employee benefits handbook, successfully directing our recruiting efforts, and establishing an on-site fitness facility."

   **If you are making a career change, you might add:** "This is a career change for me. I have always loved physical fitness and stayed in shape myself. At ABC Telecommunications, I personally purchased all the fitness equipment and encouraged our employees to use the facility. A year ago, I obtained my personal fitness certification and CPR certification. I am looking for the opportunity to work in this field."

   What will you say when asked this question?

   _____

   _____

2. **"What is one of your weaknesses?"** This is a "squirm" question that causes you to look at a negative factor about yourself. Your answer should be honest, but should not mention a severe weakness that would be critical to your current job performance. It is helpful if you have overcome this weakness or

   *(continued)*

---

*(continued)*

continually work at it. You will be seen as insincere if you can't think of a current weakness.

**A good answer:** "I am a perfectionist in terms of my work and have always met my deadlines and exceeded my sales goals. Over the years, as a sales manager and as a parent, I have learned how to motivate a wide variety of people and encourage them to excel without expecting them to meet the perfectionist standards that I set for myself. I give salespeople freedom to operate, and I have learned to measure them by their bottom-line results."

What will you say?

3. **"What does success or happiness mean to you?"** This is a tough question because of its breadth. Think about happiness in a business situation and tell the truth, but make sure the job you are applying for meets your happiness or success criteria.

**A good answer:** "As a sales professional, what makes me happy each day is feeling that I have met my new business daily-contact goals and satisfied my current customers. What makes me *extremely* happy is making a $100,000 sale and meeting my annual sales goals."

What will you say?

4. **"Where else are you interviewing?"** You can be honest here and yet not reveal the names of the companies. If you aren't interviewing with other companies, but are in the job search process, you can indicate that you have had discussions with several other companies.

**A good example:** "I am in the early stages of interviewing with two major healthcare providers in the St. Louis area."

What will you say?

5. **"Why would you want to work for us?"** This question will determine whether you have done your homework about the company or are using a scattered, shotgun approach to the interview process.

**A good answer:** "I have done my homework about your company and feel that you are on the cutting edge in terms of your assisted-living facilities. My parents are in one of your homes in Florida, and they have nothing but the highest praise for your care. Your financial statement looks good, and I would be proud to be part of your management team."

What will you say?

_____

_____

## Closing the Interview

Congratulations! You've made it through some of the toughest interview questions you'll face. It's now time to close the interview to determine where you stand. Remember this: The interview is a personal sale. Never walk away from an interview without knowing where you stand.

When you are closing the interview, don't say, "Thank you for your time. Is it okay for me to call you the first of next week?" This is a very weak approach. You will always get a yes answer, but you will not have a clear idea of how you did in the interview or how you stand in terms of receiving a job offer.

If you want this job offer, thank the interviewer for his or her time and specifically state how the company will benefit from hiring you. Then in your own words say, "Do you feel that I will be a good fit within this organization?" or "Based on our interview today, would you be prepared to recommend me for this position?"

Your interview is your personal sales presentation. You have invested time and emotional energy in it, and you are doing yourself a great disservice if you don't formally determine where you stand. The closure is one of the most critical parts of acing an interview.

## Sharpening Your Negotiation Strategies

Throughout the entire interview process, the interviewer will be asking you salary questions in the attempt to prematurely begin negotiations and hopefully hire you at the lower end of the salary scale for that position. Likewise, throughout the entire interview process, you will be building rapport with the interviewer and presenting positive information about your strengths and accomplishments in order to obtain the highest possible salary.

The most important point of career negotiation is to begin salary negotiations only when you have the complete salary and benefits package in writing and you understand the position level and responsibilities.

Don't rush things, but get your offer in writing and obtain as much information as possible in terms of the fairness of the offered salary by industry standards and the strength of your position as the lead candidate.

As you begin to compare the areas of the offer to your own expectations, take a deep breath and acknowledge that you are on better than equal footing with the employer and that most offers have some degree of flexibility. Negotiation is possible in strong and weak economies. Key areas of negotiation can include the following:

- Salary (base salary, bonuses, sign-on bonus)
- Health benefits, 401(k), stock options
- Vacation time
- Flex time
- Telecommute privileges
- Company car
- Equipment, including cell phone, laptop, pager, and PDA
- Employment contract, including severance package
- Relocation expenses
- Athletic and social club memberships and expenses
- Professional association memberships
- Tuition reimbursement

## How Does the Offer Compare to Your Needs?

Use this chart to record your desired salary and benefits and those offered. Then make notes about the areas for potential negotiation.

| Issue | Expectation | Offer | Negotiation Point |
|---|---|---|---|
| Base salary | | | |
| Bonus | | | |
| Sign-on bonus | | | |
| Vacation | | | |
| Telecommute | | | |
| Flex time | | | |
| Health benefits | | | |
| Stock options | | | |
| 401(k) | | | |
| Company car | | | |
| Equipment | | | |
| Employment contract, severance package | | | |
| Relocation expense | | | |
| Tuition reimbursement | | | |
| Athletic or social club privileges | | | |
| Professional association memberships | | | |

You'll be surprised about how many points are open for discussion and how much flexibility may be part of the original offer. Take your time and be creative and flexible. Many human resources professionals have shared with me that most job candidates never try to negotiate a job offer, although they generally have leeway in salary and benefits offers.

Also, remember that you can negotiate sign-on bonuses and other perks in a strong or weak economy. This is because these benefits may be a one-time expense to the company.

---

### To Negotiate Your Most Favorable Offer

- Begin your negotiation only after the offer has been made in writing.
- Take your time.
- Try to negotiate in person.
- Do your homework in reference to salary range.
- Determine the strength of your position as a candidate.
- Compare your expectations against the offer and negotiate the important points.
- Create a win-win agreement that benefits both sides.

---

Whether you're negotiating the offer or are still trying to get to an offer by positively answering tough interview questions (including age-related interview questions), your success depends on carefully crafting your answers and practicing them a number of times. It helps to role-play your answers with a colleague several times before an interview or negotiation session. With thorough, strategic preparation, you *will* ace the interview, avoid age discrimination, and negotiate your best offer!

---

### How Will You Prepare for Interview Questions and Salary Negotiation?

1. Which interview questions do you need to work on?

_____

_____

2. What do you need to do to prepare for a successful negotiation?

_____

_____

# CHAPTER 9

## Explore the Road Less Traveled
### Entrepreneurial Ventures and Self-Employment

*"If you do not express your own original ideas; if you do not listen to your own being; you will have betrayed yourself. Also, you will have betrayed our community in failing to make your contribution to the whole."*

—*Richard Leider and David Shapiro,* Repacking Your Bags

Your age and experience are distinct advantages to you in an entrepreneurial venture or self-employment. As an experienced worker, you possess a number of advantages over someone in the early stages of a career. Isn't it about time to have the edge?

In this chapter, we explore how you can capitalize on the advantages of your age and experience, while being alert to the traps that can snare a naïve entrepreneur.

### Affirming the Age and Experience Advantages in an Entrepreneurial/ Self-Employment Venture

Check whether these advantages apply to you:

❏ **You have in-depth work or volunteer experience and expertise in one or more areas.** (For example, Ricardo, a senior manager for a telecommunications company, had many years of technical and management experience/expertise, qualifying him to start his own telecommunications consulting business.)

❏ You have financial reserves allowing you to borrow or raise the necessary money to buy or start a business or franchise, and to sustain yourself and your family during the start-up phase. (For example, Mark bought a Bark Busters franchise and financed it with a home-equity loan. He could sustain himself through retirement savings for a year if necessary.)

❏ You have medical insurance in place for yourself and your family. (In this chapter, we explore creative ways to satisfy this need, such as working part-time or through professional associations.)

❏ You have a successful track record of goal achievement. (Following a successful history of achieving sales goals individually and in sales management in the pharmaceutical industry, Gerald bought and expanded a retirement community.)

❏ You have proven yourself to be self-directed and highly motivated and prefer taking the lead to being supervised.

❏ You are a calculated risk-taker with successful risk-taking experience in the past. You do not crave static security.

## Is There a Common Theme Among Entrepreneurs and Business Owners?

As I interview franchise owners, consultants, and those who have started or purchased businesses, I find one common theme: If you want to play in the entrepreneurial game, you have to be a risk-taker. You must be willing to sacrifice the corporate security of consistent income, health insurance, and retirement benefits for independence, time flexibility, challenge, and increased income potential.

When I interviewed Gerald, a multimillionaire owner of a retirement community, he spoke passionately about the development of his business. He said, "As an entrepreneur, you always need to stretch beyond your comfort zone. There is no middle ground; you will either succeed or flop."

Entrepreneurial ventures and self-employment can give you an opportunity to express the height of your personal self-actualization; however, with a failure rate reported to be between 50 and 77 percent, they are not for the faint of heart. In a recent survey conducted by the Chicago-based outplacement firm Challenger, Gray & Christmas, 11.4 percent of jobless managers and executives started their own businesses, up 44 percent from the preceding year. Although Challenger, Gray & Christmas did not publish a follow-up survey of the success rate of these entrepreneurial ventures, I would suspect a high failure rate from those who were "accidental entrepreneurs."

## Do You Have What It Takes to Be an Entrepreneur?

If you have experienced involuntary unemployment, you should certainly consider the option of taking the entrepreneurial route as one of many options. But you should first ask yourself whether you have what it takes to be an entrepreneur.

### Are You Entrepreneur Material?

Answering the following questions will give you an idea of whether you have the personal characteristics and financial and emotional support systems found in many successful entrepreneurs.

1. Are you self-directed, self-motivated, and disciplined?

2. Do you have strong communication skills and the ability to adapt to people with different personalities?

3. Do you have the physical and emotional stamina to devote long hours to your work?

4. Do you have financial backing or reserves, medical insurance in place, and your family's support in beginning this venture?

5. Are you good at planning, organizing, and exercising emotional control?

6. Do you have a burning desire to be an entrepreneur, or does entrepreneurship seem to be the only path available?

7. Have you researched and found a niche for your business?

8. Are you persistent in completing projects despite delays and setbacks?

9. Are you able to survive in and adapt to an unpredictable environment?

10. Do you have a significant track record of goal achievement?

If you answered "yes" to all these questions, you might have what it takes to be an entrepreneur. If you answered "yes" to at least 8 of the 10 questions, you can make it as an entrepreneur if you recognize and compensate for your weaknesses.

## What Are Your Entrepreneurial Options?

As you explore the following different entrepreneurial options, ask yourself whether you are fully committed to doing whatever it takes to make your business idea work, or will you be better off exercising your entrepreneurial talent in a corporate environment? Remember that this is always possible. Let's take a look at the variety of possibilities for entrepreneurship on the road less traveled.

- Franchises
- Consulting
- Buying an existing non-franchise business
- Starting your own business

### Exploring Franchise Ownership

A franchise is a license that a company (the franchisor) grants to a franchisee to use the company's brand name and its proven systems and procedures to build income and achieve consistency in terms of products and services. At one time I held the mistaken impressions that franchise ownership was not affordable to the average person and that most of the franchises were fast-food restaurants. Not so.

After I attended a FranNet seminar, put on by a well-respected franchise consulting firm, and had two clients and a colleague buy franchises, I learned that franchises are affordable. I also learned that the most popular franchises today include business-format franchises such as hairstyling, commercial cleaning, and so on, not just fast-food restaurants. Following are some interesting facts about franchises:

- Franchise owners do not want to work for someone else, but they do not want to develop a business from scratch.
- The average franchise costs between $30,000 and $150,000.
- Franchise owners are generally more successful than independent business owners. Eighty-five percent of all franchises succeed.
- Franchises are available in personal services, business-to-business services, retail, children's services, automotive aftermarket, and, of course, food.

## Understanding the Advantages and Disadvantages of Owning a Franchise

Using the franchise route to develop a business has five distinct advantages:

- Franchises prices are fixed and regulated by governmental disclosure requirements. You can rest assured that you are on a level playing field within your franchise.

- The franchisor provides a successful business plan, proven systems, support, and training. You don't have to reinvent the wheel. Someone else has done the hard work for you.

- Franchises can be up and running in a relatively short time.

- Franchises have a higher success rate than do new-business start-ups. This is a major advantage, given the current failure rate of new businesses.

- Franchises can be sold at a profit with the approval of the franchisor.

By this point in our lives (and we're not telling what that point is, are we?), we know that nothing is perfect. Franchising does have its disadvantages:

- The requirement to work within standardized franchise procedures can frustrate independent people.

- Some franchisees feel they don't receive sufficient support.

- Start-up costs can be high.

- Some successful franchisees resent continuing payments to the franchisor.

To sum it up, franchises are an excellent option for those who can finance a franchise and want to be formally guided in their entrepreneurial venture.

## Mining Franchise Successes

Where can you go for better information about getting into a franchise business than to those who have successfully made the transition? Listen to what two of my over-40 buddies have to say about their ventures.

## Action International (Business Consulting)

When I first met Ricardo, he had definitely decided not to play it again. He was 52 years old, had concluded a successful sales and management career for a major pharmaceutical company, and was eligible for but not interested in retirement.

I asked him why he wanted to be self-employed and he said that he had learned that there was no security in a job, only in business ownership. He described actually feeling physically ill when he thought about returning to the corporate world.

Ricardo took several career assessments, the Self-Directed Search (SDS) and the Myers-Briggs Type Indicator, and determined that consulting, teaching, and coaching were his fortes. Next he met with FranNet and researched various franchises over a three- to four-month period. Ricardo eventually bought into a franchise called Action International.

I interviewed Ricardo almost a year from our first meeting, and he was extremely happy with his choice of a business consulting franchise. He is pleased with the training, support, methods, and systems provided by his franchise management.

When I asked him about his future earnings potential, he indicated that he had awesome income potential, and would soon be having other coaches working under him. He encouraged potential franchisees to "burn their ships and take the risk." (What Ricardo was referring to is the story that when Cortez landed in the New World, he had his soldiers burn their ships, so that there would be no chance of escape. Don't take this advice literally. You *can* take calculated risks.) I know that Ricardo is an excellent promoter; he is already suggesting that he be *my* business coach!

### Bark Busters (Home Dog-Training Franchise)

I have known Mark for a number of years in a number of unusual ways. Our first meeting was at a book review discussion at Borders; our second meeting was at the Georgia Speaker's Association. Later, I invited him to be a member of my Toastmasters club, the Speakers Roundtable, and he helped me network into my position as a career-transition counselor with Right Management.

Mark and I had worked in the career-transition business together for about two years when he announced that he had bought a Bark Busters dog-training franchise. Quite frankly, I was not surprised because he has always been the adventuresome sort. In addition to that, our business constantly stimulates us with entrepreneurial career opportunities and opportunities to attend the franchise sessions conducted by FranNet.

I was interested in why Mark chose this particular franchise and his view on what it takes to be a successful franchise owner. Mark said that he chose the Bark Busters dog franchise because he loves pets and feels that services involving pets are recession proof. Mark financed the franchise with a home-equity loan, which is common in service franchises that require very few business assets. He promotes his business through veterinarians, pet boutiques, and pet stores. He has no doubt of his success after eight months in the business.

From Mark's standpoint, franchise success factors involve self-confidence and self-direction. You have to be able to do your own marketing, training, organization, and so on. If you expect the owner (franchisor) to do everything for you, you are better off working for a corporation.

Mark left me with this helpful advice shared with him by Leslie Cuban, one of the principals of FranNet: "When researching a particular franchise, talk to a franchisee who is a top player and one who is not doing as well. Ask yourself where you fit in this equation."

## Drawing Conclusions About Franchising

As I look at what successful franchise owners have in common and what makes them successful, optimism and strong interpersonal skills stand out. People enjoy being around them and doing business with them. And the franchise they have chosen allows them to express their unique personality. I think that these traits are critical ingredients for franchise success in the personal and business–to-business services arena. And, of course, in order to purchase these franchises, both Ricardo and Mark did in a figurative sense "burn their ships." They severed their corporate ties and made significant capital investments in order to finance their ventures.

*"If you have anything really valuable to contribute to the world, it will come through the expression of your own personality-that single spark of divinity that sets you off and makes you different from every other living creature."*

—*Bruce Barton*

What amazes me about some mature workers is that they will not consider franchise ownership, believing that it is too risky. On the other hand, they think nothing of spending more than $35,000 on a new car. Or they frequently lose an entire year's income or more searching for a past career position that is no longer marketable.

Go figure! The truth is that franchises have an 85 percent success rate and you can generally finance them through your bank with 10 percent down or with a home-equity loan.

Investigating franchise ownership is worth your while if you are self-directed, self-confident, optimistic, personable, and a moderate risk-taker. Take the time to do your due diligence on franchises that interest you. Research franchise opportunities online by typing "franchise opportunities" into your Internet search engine. You can research industries of interest such as beauty or education. You can contact FranNet (www.Frannet.com) in your area, and also check out other franchise opportunities online at www.entreworld.org.

## Exploring Consulting Opportunities

Consulting is the most common entrepreneurial option chosen by mature career-transition candidates. The field of consulting allows you to tap into expertise that you have developed from past career experiences or to develop new expertise in a subject of great personal interest. Start-ups are usually inexpensive, are relatively free of administrative hassles, and can be started quickly.

### Finding the Advantages and Disadvantages in Consulting

Let's take a look first at the advantages of consulting. They are amazing.

- Consulting has inexpensive start-up costs.

- You can conduct a consulting business on a full- or part-time basis.

- You can be in business quickly. Your expertise and contacts may mean that, after making a few phone calls or sending a few e-mail messages to people in your network, you can have your first piece of business.

- Your working hours can be flexible. As a consultant, you can determine when, where, and how long you work.

- Consulting offers great independence and freedom. Here is one little caveat: Independence is addictive.

Naturally, disadvantages accompany the choice to begin a consulting business:

- Consultants can make more or less than their corporate salary.

- Despite their ability to set their own schedules, consultants often work long hours and are never really through with business.

- Consultants usually work solo and do their own marketing and administrative work. Wearing multiple hats can be draining.
- Consultants have inconsistent income and must finance their own health and retirement benefits.
- A consultant's business rarely has resale value, unless it is franchised or turned into an independent business.

## Talking Shop with Successful Consultants

Now let's look at three very different consulting businesses: a speaking and corporate training business, a telecommunications consultancy, and an image-consulting business.

What do a 44-year-old mother and homemaker, a senior manager for an international telecommunications company, and an office manager and human resources liaison have in common? They each believe that their subject-matter expertise and ability to perform or deliver their services is exceptional.

## Speaking and Corporate Training

Colleen began her corporate training and speaking business when she was 44 years old, after a successful career as a mother and homemaker. Her college degree was in music education, and she knew that she had professional presentation talent. I asked her how she got started. "Did you draw up a business plan and consult with the Small Business Administration?" I know her as detailed and well organized, and this was what I expected. She confided in me that she had just stepped out without intense planning.

We talked about the advantages of the time flexibility she enjoys by working out of her virtual office. Then she bemoaned the fact that her friends and relatives don't always respect that she is really working. I share the same issues in my business.

During the course of her career, Colleen joined the prestigious National Speaker's Association. Membership requires a certain level of speaking income and testimonials from satisfied clients. Later, she became a Certified Speaking Professional (CSP), an additional testimonial to her speaking and training expertise.

I asked Colleen if she had any advice for budding entrepreneurs interested in the consulting route. Colleen suggested that not only should entrepreneurs have talent, and passion for their idea, but they should also understand the concepts of return on investment, and sales and marketing needs, before beginning their business venture. In the speaking and training business, she has seen moderately talented people who are great at sales and marketing become incredibly financially successful. She has also seen people who have great presentation talent suffer because of lack of sales and marketing expertise.

### Telecommunications Consultant Extraordinaire

Richard was a senior manager for an international telecommunications company when he was displaced because of a merger/acquisition. Instead of taking a severance package, he became their consultant for six months, which turned into a year and a half and launched his successful consulting career.

Of the consultants I interviewed, Richard is the most financially successful at this point; he has tripled his income from his corporate days. He describes himself as a telecommunications subject-matter expert. He brings new products and services to market and creates opportunities for other people as well as himself. All his business comes through networking, and he admits to spending a great deal of time on the phone. He has consulted for nine years. I asked how he establishes his fees and he indicated that he offers multiple methods: hourly, daily, and with a retainer.

When I asked him for his advice for future consultants, he said, "You must have a strong network. Cold calling won't work. Self-discipline is huge. Remember to offer the full portfolio of your skills. Also, be careful when choosing your engagements and your partners."

### Making a Fashion Statement Out of Downsizing

I first met Peggy when I notified the employees of a major Japanese manufacturing firm that they would be receiving outplacement services at Right Management. Peggy was the company's office manager and human resources liaison.

When I first met her, I was initially struck by her fashionable appearance and her vivacity. She had bright, curly, auburn hair and was attired in a rust-colored suede skirt and boots. Her makeup and hair were stylish and well done. She didn't fit my expectations of a conservatively dressed business manager.

As I got to know Peggy better, she confided that she had always loved fashion and that she considered her downsizing as the perfect opportunity to develop her business as an image consultant.

During the time she was using our outplacement services, she attended all our classes. Peggy read every image book that she could get her hands on, and investigated associations and classes in image consulting. Before she officially started her own business, she had scored her first client by word of mouth at her gym. And, as a result of our conversations, she was kind enough to do makeovers for a number of our career-transition clients attending a career fair. Peggy's before-and-after pictures are found in Chapter 7.

Peggy completed a well-known advanced image-consulting class in Atlanta that included a week of 11-hour days and a certification and is a member of the Association of Image Consultants International. I have absolutely no doubt of her future success because of her talent, drive, and outgoing personality. She has joined a local Toastmasters club and is marketing herself by speaking to women's clubs and heavily networking.

When you are developing a consulting business, obtaining credentials will add to your credibility, such as Peggy's Certified Image Consultant status and Colleen's Certified Speaking Professional designation.

## Drawing Conclusions About Consulting

When I look at what successful consultants have in common, I find many of the same characteristics of successful franchise owners. These consultants have strong interpersonal skills, overtly expressed in their business, and they are optimistic. But, they are not as willing to "burn their boats" in terms of financial risk-taking.

From my vantage point, the differences between franchisees and consultants involve level of risk and level of self-esteem. Consultants are mild risk-takers. They want independence, but not initial financial risk. Because they are the product, their self-esteem must be high in order for them to succeed. In a franchise, your self-esteem must be high, but your product is not yourself. The financial reward factor can be equally high for both, but generally the consultant's business has no resale value.

# Exploring Buying an Existing Non-Franchise Business

As we explore the possibility of buying an existing business, the stakes and the risk involved often increase dramatically. The business owners I interviewed heard about these businesses accidentally from an associate or friend, while they were still employed. They indicated to me that advertised businesses could be suspect because "why would someone want to sell a thriving business?"

Despite their warning, I was sure that there were reliable places to go to find independent businesses for sale. Here are some of the sources I discovered.

- **Business brokers:** You can type "business broker" into a search engine, along with your city or state of interest, and find businesses for sale. You can also locate business brokers in the *Yellow Pages,* some with industry specialties. Remember that brokers represent the buyer, so you must do your own due diligence and get professional help in examining the financials and legal issues involved.

- **Businesses for sale:** www.bizology.com is an interesting site where independent businesses are offered for sale. Businesses are categorized by area of interest such as hospitality, consulting, auto repair, and so on. An online course offers a 200-point due diligence checklist, and book testimonials are convincing. Entrepreneurial magazines such as *Inc.* and *Entrepreneur* also advertise businesses for sale, and your local newspaper will also have listings.

### Finding the Advantages and Disadvantages in Buying a Business

Nearly every entrepreneurial option has advantages, or no one would be choosing it. The advantages to purchasing an existing business are

- The existing business can be running well and be profitable. You can just step into its success without experiencing the delay of income and rocky beginning a brand-new business usually experiences.

- The owner might be willing to participate in the financing and provide training and support as in a franchise.

- You can participate in the day-to-day operations as much as you desire. If you are a hands-on person, you can jump right in and get to work. If you'd like a more relaxed schedule, you frequently can use the existing staff and operations that are in place and are proven winners.

- Buying an existing successful business gives you an immediate, solid income potential. Who doesn't like that?
- You can franchise your business, leave it to your heirs, or sell it for a profit.

Are there disadvantages to buying an existing business? Yes, if you are a naïve buyer and don't do your due diligence.

- Although you can use the services of a business broker (a company that specializes in selling businesses), there is no organized buying market. You will need to conduct major research to locate a business, research its financials, and negotiate its purchase.
- Because each independent business is unique, the government has not created standard financial disclosure requirements. You are on your own, so it's good to have a lawyer and an accountant analyze a prospective deal.
- Financing is difficult unless you have experience in the business area or the business has an intrinsic value such as land and capital equipment.
- The transaction costs of buying a business are higher, and the time it takes to close the deal is longer than those accompanying a franchise purchase.
- An existing business comes with no formal support mechanism. You might want to negotiate an arrangement with the current owner for a cooperative transition period. After that, you're on your own.

## Taking Heart from a Business-Buying Success

Buying an existing business can be tricky. It can also be lucrative. Don't take my word for it. Listen to what this former district sales manager of pharmaceuticals has to say.

Gerald had a successful career as a district sales manager for a major pharmaceutical firm, but had always wanted to own his own business. I asked him if this was the American Dream? He said that he didn't know about it being everyone's dream, but he remembered his mother admiring people who owned their own business, and it was his dream.

Gerald stumbled upon the opportunity to buy a retirement community with manufactured homes. A friend partnered with him, and he left the comfort and security of his corporate career for the precipice of business ownership, where he would either reach a summit or plummet.

I asked him about the financials of buying a business. Did he hire a CPA and lawyer, or go to great extent to make sure the business was well valued? He said he didn't. Their first business plan was written on a cocktail napkin, but the land in the retirement community had intrinsic value, and they were able to borrow the money they needed to buy it and develop it. The amount they borrowed was in the millions. Gerald said, "You will succeed if there is no safety blanket." He had to pay his notes as they came due, and he did not have a year's reserve of income in the bank. He did have the support of a loving family.

Eventually Gerald bought out his partner and the park of 30 spaces now has 195 spaces. He is incredibly financially successful.

### Drawing Conclusions About Buying an Existing Non-Franchise Business

Buying an existing business can involve greater risk than buying a franchise or being self-employed as a consultant. On the other hand, it has the greatest potential for financial gain, right up there with starting your own business.

Successful independent business owners are personable, are optimistic, and have high self-esteem. They usually have previous success in sales or management. Their ability to take risk is high, and they are willing to "burn their boats."

## Exploring Starting Your Own Business

You can see from the entrepreneurial options we have covered that when people express the desire to own their own business, they might mean franchise ownership, consulting, or buying an existing business. On the other hand, they really could mean starting their own business.

Starting your own business from scratch can be the most difficult entrepreneurial venture because you have no model to follow of proven systems and procedures. On top of that, the failure rate is high—sources claim between 50 and 77 percent. And you often have no intrinsic value of land, buildings, or equipment to put up as collateral for a loan. But, starting your own business can be a satisfying and lucrative choice. Let's take a look at the advantages and disadvantages of starting your own business.

### Finding the Advantages and Disadvantages in Starting Your Own Business

With so many people dreaming of owning their own businesses, you know that there must be advantages to doing so. Just what are they? Take a look at this list of three:

- Self-actualization, the opportunity to develop your "big idea," and doing it your way are all advantages of starting your own business. The independent person often can't resist the urge to be the next self-made millionaire.

- Start-ups offer the possibility of large business returns. Some say that the greater the risk, the greater the potential for wealth.

- Your business has future value to expand, to franchise, to sell, and to pass on to your heirs. You are carving a space for your business into the economic landscape. The future of your business is in your hands.

Given the reported failure rate of starting your own business, there must be some major disadvantages. They are the following:

- You are developing your own business model from scratch. Notice that this point can be an advantage or a disadvantage. The only difference is the perspective of the business owner. A risk-taker enjoys the challenge; a play-it-safer might quake at all that lies ahead.

- Start-ups offer significant risk and are often difficult to finance because of lack of capital. You have to convince your investors that your business idea will succeed.

- Start-ups often consume an excessive commitment of time and energy. Do you have plenty of both? Your age is not the determining factor; neither is your vision. Listen to your body and your support network on this one.

- Financial success takes a number of years. You must have a plan for getting through the lean years.

### Gaining Hope from a Start-up Business Pro

When are you too old to start a business? If you believe the example of Tom, the answer to this age question is just a matter of mindset.

When I heard that one of our career-transition clients had started his own bank, I knew that I had to interview him, and his story did not disappoint me. It speaks to the power and energy of a mature entrepreneur.

When Tom retired from a major bank at 62, he was the President of Institutional Trusts and Investments. Four months into his career transition and with no intention of retiring, he had a conversation with one of his son's college friends who wanted to start a bank and had five years of entrepreneurial and fund-raising experience, but no banking experience. The two men clicked and began what would be a two-year partnership process of organizing and funding a new local bank through individual investors. This was a multimillion-dollar funding project.

When I spoke with Tom, he was excited, dedicated, and fully involved. What we both shared is the importance of not letting your age be an issue in your entrepreneurship venture. Tom reminded me of millionaires he knew that had built their businesses after age 65. And I shared that many mature workers are young and energetic in their 70s, and other workers are physically and mentally old and apathetic in their 30s. Age on paper has little to do with age in action.

*"Youth is not a time of life; it is a state of mind."*

—*Samuel Ulman*

### Drawing Conclusions About Starting a Business

Successful self-made business owners are extremely risk tolerant, have strong interpersonal skills, and overtly express their personalities in their work. Their distinguishing personality trait is that they, like consultants, feel that their product or service is the "best on the block." They also feel that they can "do it better" than anyone else.

If you are considering starting your own independent business, use the wisdom of your age and experience to consider the pros and cons before taking the leap. Not all new businesses are "giant leaps." The following chart shows the risk and reward factors of each type of business.

## Risk and Reward Factors

| Type of Business | Risk Factor | Reward Factor |
|---|---|---|
| Franchise Ownership | Moderate | Medium High |
| Consulting | Mild | Moderate to Medium High |
| Buying an Existing Business | Moderate to High | High |
| Starting a New Business | High | High |

### All Free Advice Is Not Bad Advice

After you have decided to pursue your business idea in terms of a franchise, consulting opportunity, or buying or starting a new business, you will need a business plan, support, and a business entity. The United States Small Business Administration offers online and in-person free support. The Small Business Administration has a group of retired executives, SCORE, who will serve as mentors to you in the early phases of your business, so why go it alone?

# What Legal Business Entity Should You Use?

Clients frequently ask me whether they should form a sole proprietorship, Chapter C or S, or an LLC. In the following sections, you will find helpful information on which legal entity/type of business is appropriate for you.

## Sole Proprietorships

There are many advantages to choosing a sole proprietor business (ownership) model. It is quick, uncomplicated, and inexpensive. Usually, you do not have to file documents with your state, but you might need a license—if it is required by your state. There are no legal start-up costs and little administration. The main drawbacks are that your personal assets might be used to pay back business debt, and your liability is unlimited.

I have always had a sole proprietorship and have no business debt or legal liability issues, so this has been a good model for me. If you are a sole proprietor, you are the only owner, but you can have a business with multiple streams of income such as training, consulting, writing, and so on. Bill Elemeyer, a senior vice president with Lee Hecht Harrison, a well-known outplacement firm, was recently interviewed in the *Orange County Register*. He describes his own business as career transition, executive coaching, professional speaking, and marketing consulting. Bill expressed the belief that people with solid work experience should be able to sculpt their skills into a solid portfolio of self-employment.

## General Partnerships

General partnerships share most of the pluses and minuses of sole proprietorship. On the plus side, two or more owners share business responsibilities. On the minus side, all partners are responsible for the debts and business-related actions of the other partner. They also share unlimited liability. Therefore, it is very important that detailed partnership agreements are drawn up to clarify as many liability and responsibility issues as possible before the business is in place.

## Corporations

There are three types of corporations: C, S, and LLC. The following chart shows the basic differences that you should investigate in detail before making a choice. All three are separate legal entities.

My career clients frequently ask me about setting up a corporation even before they have a "big idea" envisioned or a business plan in place. I believe that you should not do business until you have established the legal structure of your new organization, but it is folly to agonize over the business structure before you have a "big idea" and a business plan in place. Also, continue to ask yourself whether you have the personal characteristics and support to be an entrepreneur. If you do, continue your exploration and get started.

# How Does Entrepreneurship Fit in with Future Employment Trends?

Those of us in outplacement, staffing, and recruiting have seen the shift from full-time employment to project management and temporary staffing. I can see a dynamic future expansion of this trend. Also, companies continue to outsource technology and manufacturing overseas where labor is cheaper. What this means for you as a corporate worker is less job security, which makes entrepreneurial ventures more interesting. Also, don't forget the quasi-entrepreneurial

## A Comparison of Types of Corporations

| Type | Ownership | Advantages | Disadvantages | Taxes |
|------|-----------|------------|---------------|-------|
| Subchapter C | Unlimited shareholders | ▪ Limited liability<br>▪ Company-paid fringe benefits<br>▪ Capital easy to raise through stock sales | ▪ Costly to form<br>▪ Administrative duties<br>▪ Taxation on corporate earnings and individual dividends | Corporation pays its own |
| Subchapter S | Limited to 35 shareholders | ▪ Limited liability<br>▪ No double taxation (shareholders report income on individual tax returns) | ▪ Costly to form<br>▪ Administrative duties | Paid by owner/owners |
| LLC | Owned by members | ▪ Limited liability<br>▪ No double taxation<br>▪ Less paperwork | ▪ Ownership hard to transfer | Taxed as a partnership or corporation |

self-employment possibilities. For example, a self-employed massage therapist works several days a week at Starbucks for medical and 401(k) benefits, and the spouse of a new-business start-up entrepreneur works at Barnes & Noble a few days a week for the same reason. Another option to investigate: The National Small Business Association, www.nsbahealth.com, also offers medical insurance plans.

## Which Road Will You Choose?

As you can see from these wonderful entrepreneurial examples, some people dive right in and plan their business on a cocktail napkin. Others spend months in due diligence and investigation. There is no right or wrong way to get started. It's just important to get started, to make your dream a reality. And don't let a negative attitude about your age get in the way of your success.

Why do you want to start a business at your age? Why don't you just sit back, relax, and have a margarita on the patio?

I love working. I feel energized about the prospect of starting my own business!

*Negative Stereotype: Your energy is low and your brain is slow.*

## What Road Will You Take?

As you consider your entrepreneurial options, take time to choose a venture that truly expresses your "ideal" career. When your interests, abilities, marketability, earnings, values, and lifestyle preferences are fed, your choice has made all the difference.

*"Two roads diverged in a wood, and I—I took the one less traveled by, and that has made all the difference."*

—Robert Frost, *"The Road Not Taken"*

1. Make a list of the type(s) of businesses that interest you.

_____     _____

_____     _____

2. List the franchise opportunities in these businesses.

_____     _____

_____     _____

3. List interesting businesses for sale on the Internet or through a business broker.

_____     _____

_____     _____

4. What is your area of interest or expertise that could become an opportunity to consult or have your own business?

_____

_____

# CHAPTER 10

## Too Young to Quit Working
### Careers for Post-Retirement Years

*"Retirement has been redefined. It is no longer an automatic shift in gears from work to non-work at a set age. It is, rather, a voluntary withdrawal from the work force at the age that best suits an individual's abilities, interests, and career plans."*

—The End of Mandatory Retirement, *Walker and Lazer*

Fifteen years ago, my brother-in-law Bob told me that he never expected to retire. I thought, "that is ridiculous. Why would someone want to continue working in their 60s and 70s unless they were in financial need?" My own plans were to retire at 55 from a highly compensated corporate sales management job, to enjoy family and friends, and to travel to exotic international destinations. Little did I know that when I reached 55, I would be saying, "Forget about retirement. I'll work as long as I want. I can work and still enjoy family, friends, and travel to exotic international destinations."

### When Is the Right Age to Quit Working?

The question is not really "When is the right age to quit working," but "what work do you want to do at your current age?" Mandatory retirement was widespread in the 1960s and 1970s, but in 1978 the U.S. Congress outlawed mandatory retirement before age 70, and in 1986 abolished it altogether. Authorities indicate that this extension of the Age Discrimination in Employment Act

(ADEA) was brought about to raise labor force participation and to create a more flexible definition of retirement. Unfortunately, many older workers and potential employers have not bought into this flexible definition of retirement. Some employers still engage in subtle and not-so-subtle age discrimination, and a few older workers engage in *self*-discrimination by entertaining negative thoughts about their age, their career choice, what others will say, and so on.

*Negative Stereotype: I will be a cultural misfit because of my age.*

A recent survey by AARP indicates that 23 percent of us will be working after we reach 70 because of a variety of reasons: increased financial need, based on declining 401(k)s and the fact that we are living longer; and the desire to stay mentally and physically fit, to be productive, and to enjoy ourselves. You really have no reason to retire unless you want to. The ages of 55, 60, 65, 70, or even 75 are only arbitrary numbers that have increasingly less significance in today's world where couples start families in their 30s and 40s and we are experiencing an exponential increase in the number of centenarians (people over 100). Life seems to be starting later and continuing longer.

The number of centenarians in the United States is doubling every decade. According to the U.S. Census Bureau, the United States had 70,000 centenarians in 1999, and projections are that the number will rise to 834,000 by 2050. You may be one of them. For projections on how long you will live, check out www.livingto100.com. I took the quiz and found out that I may live to be 113.7 years, so I am even more motivated to keep working. I also discovered that I needed to work on my stress management and drink green tea.

Your actual age number has little significance in your "ageless" employment status, but what does have significance is that you choose work that supports your emerging preferences and values. For some people, making a certain annual income will be a continuing necessity; for others, time flexibility or being involved in meaningful paid or unpaid work is critical.

You will be more content in your career choices if you incorporate your preferences and values. Take a moment to complete the following worksheet for some real eye openers.

## Rating Your Preferences and Values

First, rank these preferences and values on a scale of 1 to 10, with 1 being the most important to you. Feel free to have more than one of the same value. Next circle your top three.

| Career Preference/Value | Fulfillment Score |
| --- | --- |
| High income potential | |
| Time flexibility | |
| Opportunity for recognition/ encouragement/approval | |
| Opportunity to contribute/ give back/provide meaning | |
| Opportunity for self-expression/ input/creativity | |
| Benefits: medical/retirement | |
| Career autonomy/empowerment/choice | |

*(continued)*

*(continued)*

Expression of existing strengths/
interests/abilities

Development of new competencies

Challenge/stimulation/learning

Activity/action/fun/variety

Stability/affiliation/teamwork

Power/leadership/responsibilities

Not physically challenging

Other:

When you are evaluating job or career opportunities or considering self-employment, use your top three preferences/values to determine whether the potential opportunity fulfills what you consider most important. You will eliminate later disappointments by honoring your personal preferences and values.

## Evaluating Some of the Best Retirement Career Options

By now, you've learned that the term "retirement careers" is an oxymoron in itself, but does has some merit in describing those careers we choose after we are 55, 60, 65, or even 70. The best retirement career options are those that match your preferences and values. Many different mature career options are available, and the following list groups them in four categories:

- Corporate or organizational employment: full-time, part-time, and contract

- Temporary and seasonal employment

- Self-employment, including franchises, business ownership, and consulting opportunities

- Volunteer opportunities

Each category has its merits depending on your own preferences and values. In fact, you may want to combine several of these categories into a new category: concurrent employment. This fast-growing employment trend can be a combination of jobs from two or more of the preceding categories. For example, Dick, a self-employed CPA, works part-time from his home office as a consultant and volunteers as a SCORE counselor for the Small Business Administration.

## Corporate or Organizational Employment

Believe it or not, many people love their corporate or organizational full-time employment and never want to leave. Such a person is my cousin Jane, who has been playing bass in the Atlanta Symphony since she was a teenager. At 75, she has no plans to retire and is going for a spot in the Guinness Book of World Records as the symphony member of a major orchestra with the longest career. If you love your work and can keep up, why not stay with it?

For most of us who want time flexibility, medical benefits, or action and fun, a part-time or contract position may be made-to-order. Seniors who seek fresh challenges will find employers glad to help them out. According to a recent survey by the Society for Human Resource Management, 68 percent of employers said they hire retirees as consultants or temporary workers. In fact, SunTrust Bank, Starbucks, and the IRS offer medical benefits for some part-time positions. Starbucks offers benefits at 20 hours of work.

Many companies enjoy hiring former employees for part-time or contract work. Stan had been a successful outside insurance sales professional for a major insurance brokerage. He contacted the company about the possibility of doing promotional work for them. Instead of doing promotional work, he landed a research contract to identify and obtain full sales lead information involving major Southeast businesses with $1,000,000 and over in sales in selected industries. This contract work was quite a challenge with a tight deadline, involving the need to separate all leads by their offices and to record the information in Excel spreadsheets. Stan hired two people to help him with clerical and research tasks. The project came in on time, and he made a bonus for his efforts.

I asked Stan to rate his contract and part-time insurance assignment in terms of his preferences and values. The following table lists Stan's values and rates the project in terms of those values.

## Corporate or Organizational Employment: Contract or Part-Time

| Stan's Career Preferences/Values | Corporate or Organizational Employment: Contract or Part-time | Fulfillment Score |
|---|---|---|
| High income potential | Depends on the job | #1 |
| Time flexibility | No | 10 |
| Opportunity for recognition/ encouragement/approval | Yes, and bonus | 10 |
| Opportunity to contribute/ give back/provide meaning | Depends on the job | 5 |
| Opportunity for self-expression/ input/creativity | Depends on the job | 5 |
| Benefits: medical/retirement | In some cases | 0 |
| Career autonomy/ empowerment/choice | Depends on the job | #3 |
| Expression of existing strengths/ interests/abilities | Yes | 8 |
| Development of new competencies | Yes | 8 |
| Challenge/stimulation/learning | Yes | #2 |
| Activity/action/fun/variety | Yes | 9 |
| Stability/affiliation/teamwork | No | 0 |
| Power/leadership/responsibilities | Depends on the job | #1 |
| Not physically challenging | Depends on the job | 4 |
| Other: | | |

Stan confided in me that he had enjoyed many contract assignments with his old firm, but this was not one of them. He had autonomy and power and was well paid, but the deadline and the need to push his subcontractors made it a nightmare experience. Stan's top three values are

1. Self-expression and creativity
2. Expression of strengths, interests, and abilities
3. Time flexibility

But, as you can see from his ratings of this contract assignment, Stan's top three values were not fulfilled in this assignment. He admits that his desire for fast money caused him to take an assignment he should have passed on.

In considering working in a corporate environment on a contract or part-time basis, make sure that the opportunity represents an expression of your three most important values.

What if you are not sure what you want to do but want some career stimulation? Check out three Web sites for seniors:

- www.seniors4hire.org
- www.seniorjobbank.org
- www.aarp.org

I found jobs on these sites that I would have sought if I did not have my own career-transition business. One of the advantages of being in what some are calling "the third age" is that you don't have to work at any one career longer than you enjoy it. You can be a dilettante and change careers. Or you can work at multiple careers at the same time, what I call concurrent careers.

## Temporary and Seasonal Employment

Two years ago, I volunteered to do a career workshop at a local church. As we were doing preparatory work for the employment experience section of our resumes, Laura said she had a problem: For the last seven years, she had two or three different employers a year. At first, I was astounded and thought that she had been jumping employers or had been terminated. At that time, I had been working with more traditional corporate clients and had not yet experienced the growing phenomenon of older workers who consistently work in temporary and seasonal employment.

Laura was 56 years old and was professionally trained as a dental assistant. After she divorced and moved to another city, she was tired of the dental assistant occupation and began selecting temporary and seasonal employment as she found it. This year Laura had worked for the IRS as a data-entry clerk during tax season and at the Crowne Plaza hotel as a special events bartender during the Christmas season and for parties. She is consistently independently employed as an elder caregiver, and works as a small-business office assistant when needed. Let's take a look at how these temporary and seasonal positions fulfill her preferences and values.

As you look at the chart on Laura's seasonal and temporary work, ask yourself whether this option meets your career preferences and values. For Laura, the cons are the lack of benefits and the fact that working long hours is physically demanding.

You can make as much income in seasonal and temporary work as in some full-time work in a corporate environment if you are willing to work long hours. Or, you can supplement your retirement income or Social Security income by working a more limited number of hours. As to whether this is a good retirement option for later years, I would say it depends on your physical endurance, mental agility, and personal aspirations. I do not see Laura working 80 hours a week after she is 65. I see her socking her money away, investing well, and considerably reducing her hours.

You can also find numerous temporary employment opportunities if you have good computer, writing, sales, and project-management skills. Check out www.tjobs.com and www.net-temps.com to connect with temporary employment agencies that you can find in the *Yellow Pages* and on the Internet.

## Self-Employment

Chapter 9 looked at entrepreneurial possibilities, including franchise ownership, consulting, speaking, training, buying a business, and starting your own business. These options are also a possibility for your post-retirement career plans.

Of a group of 15 to 20 flexible career counselors at a well-known career transition firm, at least 75 percent are also self-employed as consultants and in other concurrent positions that support personal preferences and values. The median age is 55, and some consultants have continued to work into their 70s.

## Temporary and Seasonal Employment Career Options

| Career Preference/Value | Temporary and Seasonal Employment | Fulfillment Score |
| --- | --- | --- |
| High Income Potential | Moderate, but you can work many hours and receive overtime at $10–15 per hour | #1 |
| Time flexibility | No, unless you take time off | 10 |
| Opportunity for recognition/encouragement/approval | Yes | 6 |
| Opportunity to contribute/give back/provide meaning | Yes, depending on assignment | #2 |
| Opportunity for self-expression/input/creativity | Not often | 9 |
| Benefits: Medical/retirement | No, except IRS provides medical benefits opportunity | 0 |
| Career autonomy/empowerment/choice | Not frequently | 8 |
| Expression of existing strengths/interests/abilities | Depends on the job | 5 |
| Development of new competencies | Yes, if you select new challenge | 4 |
| Challenge/stimulation/learning | Yes, depending on the job | 4 |
| Activity/action/fun/variety | Yes, with multiple jobs; but some are boring | #3 |
| Stability/affiliation/teamwork | Not consistently | 9 |
| Power/leadership/responsibility | Depends on the job | 8 |
| Not physically demanding | Depends on the job | 8 |

I have noticed an employment and a gradual unemployment pattern. When consultants are first employed, they frequently opt for a 40-plus-hour week. As they become older and more experienced, they seem to become less satisfied with a 9-to-6 workweek and go to a four-day week or less. This trend seems to be natural and positive. You don't have to quit. Just reduce your corporate work hours when you want to pursue your own business or hobbies.

Eleanor was a career-transition consultant and an excellent presenter in her 50s who taught a course titled "Entrepreneurship." Eleanor went from a five-day workweek to a four-day week, and then moved to North Carolina to pursue her dream of being part of and living in a spiritual/healing community. When she left, she remarked to me, "I have been encouraging others to pursue their dream. Now it's time for me to pursue my own."

It has been 11 months since Eleanor left her corporate career to pursue self-employment. She intentionally retained her corporate connection part-time but shifted her emphasis to her life- and career-coaching business. Reducing her work hours before she moved gave her time to incubate and to tap into what she really wanted to do.

What Eleanor didn't realize when she moved to a somewhat rural community in North Carolina was that her life- and career-coaching business would be harder to build outside of a major city. Her community has many retirees, and few business and professional clubs and associations. Opportunities to promote her business are 45 to 55 minutes away. For the moment, she is relying on former clients, networking, word of mouth, and doing most of her coaching over the phone and by e-mail. She is in the process of developing a formal advertising campaign, including brochures, Web site, and newspaper advertisements.

Eleanor's advice to the budding entrepreneur is this: "Starting a business takes a lot longer than you might expect. Do as much as possible while you are working part-time to ease the financial drain and enable you to get on your feet sooner."

Let's take a look at how self-employment has fulfilled Eleanor's values and preferences: Her top three values and preferences are rated and shaded, and all other career preference values are rated, with 1 being her top preference/value and 10 being her least.

## Self-Employment Career Options

| Career Preference/Value | Self-Employment | Fulfillment Score |
|---|---|---|
| High income potential | Yes, if pursued | 4 |
| Time flexibility | Yes | 4 |
| Opportunity for recognition/ encouragement/approval | Yes, if needed | 0 (not required) |
| Opportunity to contribute/ give back/provide meaning | Yes | #2 |
| Opportunity for self-expression/ input/creativity | Yes | #1 |
| Benefits: medical/retirement | None, but can supplement by partial corporate employment | 0 (not required) |
| Work autonomy/empowerment/choice | More than corporate, but consumer and client driven | 0 (not required) |
| Expression of strengths/interests/abilities | Yes | #3 |
| Development of new competencies | Yes | 4 |
| Challenge/stimulation/learning | Yes | 5 |
| Activity/action/fun/variety | Yes | 6 |
| Stability/affiliation/teamwork | Moderate | 0 (not required) |
| Power/leadership/responsibility | Yes | 0 (not required) |
| Not physically demanding | Yes | 5 |

As you review the chart on self-employment career options, ask yourself whether this option meets your top three preferences and values. Remember that you can be self-employed and fulfill different values and options than Eleanor.

## Volunteer Opportunities

It is wonderful to think of the wide range of volunteer jobs/activities available for those who no longer need income. You have probably heard seniors say, "I'm busier now than when I was working full time." So what are they doing?

Jan is an example of a senior who is really enjoying herself. She is one of my friends who has been retired from her profession as an environmental engineer for five years. She has astutely managed her investments with the help of her brother, a financial planner, and does not have ongoing financial needs to fund through employment. I remember asking her at our last lunch together, "What are you doing with your time?"

"Well, I'm painting a nursery in my home for my new grandchild. The ceiling is the worst! And I'm planning my next birthday party. It's another big one! I'm planning on having a band and lots of good food."

When I asked Jan about her volunteer activities, I found out that she volunteers in five different activities: She tutors an inner-city child several days a week, started a butterfly garden for the school, has become a Master Gardner, volunteers at her church, and volunteers for the native plant society. All in all, she spends at least a day a week in volunteer activities. Sounds like a busy life! Jan has a wide cadre of friends and also travels extensively. Jan is a cancer survivor who knows that life is precious, and each day has special meaning.

When I asked Jan and Wayne, another friend, for their experiential advice on volunteer opportunities, they said to choose those that relate to your areas of interest, preference, and values. Both are interested in nature and community service. I also asked both what career they would choose if their financials changed and they needed an income. Jan said that she would do landscape consulting. Although she cannot advertise her Master Gardner status, she has already provided this service as part of a church auction. Wayne indicated that he would be a paid naturalist and canoe guide on the Chattahoochee River.

## Volunteering Opportunities Recommended by Jan and Wayne

- Volunteer tutoring in reading and ESL (English as a second language) opportunities
- Spontaneous volunteering for friends in need
- Mission opportunities through a church
- Providing meals at a local homeless shelter
- Volunteering as a nature guide
- Volunteering as a member of a native plant society
- Working to increase voter registration

Let's see how Jan's preferences and values are expressed in her volunteer work.

## Volunteer Opportunities

| Career Preference/Value | Volunteer Opportunities | Fulfillment Score |
|---|---|---|
| High income potential | None | 0 |
| Time flexibility | Yes | 6 |
| Opportunity for recognition/ encouragement/approval | Can be informal | 8 |
| Opportunity to contribute/ give back/provide meaning | Yes | #1 |
| Opportunity for self-expression/ input/creativity/ | Yes | 9 |
| Benefits: medical/retirement | No | 0 |
| Career autonomy/ empowerment/choice | Yes | 9 |
| Expression of existing strengths/ interests/abilities | Yes | #2 |
| Development of new competencies | Yes | 4 |
| Challenge/stimulation/learning | Yes | #6 |

*(continued)*

(continued)

| | | |
|---|---|---|
| Activity/action/fun/variety | Yes | #3 |
| Stability/affiliation/teamwork | Yes | #7 |
| Power/leadership/responsibilities | No | 0 |
| Not physically challenging | Depends | 5 |
| Other: | | |

As you rank your career preferences and values, remember that yours will be different from Jan's.

Volunteer activities are listed weekly in the newspapers. You can search for opportunities online by typing the keywords "volunteer activities," along with your city name, into your favorite search engine. Two Web sites I recommend are www.servenet.org, and for international opportunities, www.crossculturalsolutions.org.

# Enjoying a Career in Your "Third Stage of Life"

A career in the years after your 55th birthday can be the most satisfying time of your entire life. It's a time for self-assessment; a time to pause and evaluate how your preferences and values will play out in a corporate or organizational environment, in self-employment, and in volunteer work.

You have the opportunity to excel at any age and be increasingly accepted in many employment and organizational venues. Not only can you make money to support the lifestyle you desire, but you can also self-actualize again and again and again, reinventing yourself and fulfilling lifelong dreams. You can change careers or you can have multiple concurrent careers. It's up to you.

According to Ronald Kotulak in *Inside the Brain: Revolutionary Discoveries of How the Mind Works* (Andrews McMeel), people do not lose massive numbers of brain cells as they age. The brain's functions simply get rusty with disuse. He describes a number of well-documented research studies that indicate that keeping your mental fires ablaze is within your control.

Employment and volunteer activities can provide many of these brain stimulants:

- Reading
- Engaging in age-appropriate strenuous physical activity
- Traveling
- Participating in cultural events
- Engaging in continuous education
- Participating in clubs and professional associations
- Gaining satisfaction from accomplishments
- Showing willingness to change
- Feeling that what you do makes a difference in the lives of others

Jeff, 53, owner of Corporate Comedy and one of my business partners in the corporate training aspect of my business, regenerates himself in his work. When we travel together, he is not in his room, mindlessly zonking out on TV, but is practicing Tai Chi to increase his balance, and painting difficult Chinese brushstroke bamboo to stimulate his brain. On the same trip, you will find me painting folk art animals and walking and running four miles. (Heh, I'm not telling *my* age.)

In one of my seminars, I challenge participants to consider their future work/lifestyle by asking questions. One of the questions I asked was this:

> If you could choose the most exciting/glamorous career, what would you choose?

I posed this question to one of my older clients who was trying to figure out what he wanted to do next. He said that he wanted be a paid naturalist. He is a volunteer naturalist now at the Chattahoochee Nature Center. His glamour version of a paid naturalist is to lead exotic adventure trips. After talking for an hour or so, we decided that he would start with outdoor adventure canoe trips. These plans justify his recent purchase of a third canoe and a cool new pair of water sandals.

You are never too old to adopt a version of your dream. One of my very wise friends, Susan, a psychologist, encourages us to look for the essence of what we want. Wayne wanted to lead exotic adventure trips. These trips didn't have to begin on the Amazon, but could start at a river landing three miles from his home. Think about how you can achieve the essence of what you want. Do something immediately to support your dream.

## What Is Your Impossible Dream?

Take a quiet moment and answer these questions for yourself for a preview of future possibilities:

1. If you were beginning your career all over again, what career would you choose?

_____

2. If you no longer had financial need, what would you do as a career or volunteer activity?

_____

3. If you had no physical or age limitations, what career would you choose?

_____

4. If you could choose the most exciting or glamorous career, what would you choose?

_____

5. What is the first way that you will manifest your dream?

_____

# EPILOGUE

## Ongoing Job Search and Career Management

### Easing the Financial Drain of Career Search and the Emotional Roller-Coaster of Career Management

As I sat across from Don at the circular table in my office, I noticed that he was wringing his hands and had a crestfallen look on his face. He had been out of work for over a year and felt that he would be facing financial meltdown in two months if he was not employed.

Don is an example of what not to do. He waited until the last minute to seek emergency career advice. He did not take advantage of the outplacement services provided by his former employer, or seek paid or free career counseling. He was proud and overly self-sufficient.

Fortunately, Don and I did some very fast career redirection, and he was reemployed within two months. Don put himself and his family under a lot of unnecessary emotional and financial stress that you can avoid.

### Avoiding Unnecessary Financial Stress

When you are unemployed, career counselors routinely tell you, "Your job is to find a job." This means that you should be diligent in your job search for the career you desire. What they should be saying to you is this: "Your job is to find a job and avoid unnecessary financial drain. If you cannot locate or create an acceptable job before your severance runs out, and your living expenses are beginning to eat into your retirement, take a less than perfect job or two less than perfect jobs so that you can pay your basic personal and family expenses." You can search for your ideal job while you are employed. This happens all the time.

Four blind spots can cause you to overextend your career search time and cause serious financial drain:

- Unrealistic status expectations
- Unrealistic salary expectations
- Career tunnel vision
- Reluctance to apply for unemployment compensation

The following sections discuss each of these blind spots.

## Unrealistic Status Expectations

By the time you are 40, 50, 60, or older, you may be justly proud of your career achievements. You have a wealth of valuable work and volunteer experience. You may be titled—not royally but as a corporate officer, a JD (attorney), a SPHR (Senior Professional in Human Resources), and so on. Over the years, you have achieved a certain status that feels good, feeds your ego, and enhances your self-esteem. But an unrealistic expectation of maintaining your past status as the required status quo can cause you to shoot yourself in the foot.

For two years, Robert, aged 58, tried unsuccessfully to replace his position as a vice president in telecommunications. Although he had two small consulting opportunities within this time, he failed to explore other career opportunities soon enough. He continued to feel that they were beneath him, and he was trying to preserve his status as Vice President of Telecommunications.

Two years is a long time to be out of work, especially when you are the only breadwinner and you have developed an expensive lifestyle. Robert was forced to sell his Jaguar and his vacation home. He also significantly cannibalized his retirement savings before he took a job selling high-end cars.

Robert's status expectations got in his way. He didn't realize soon enough that his mature age and economic conditions were working against him. Robert should have sought professional career help, read career guides, taken temporary work early on, and continued his job search or retooled himself for another career.

If you are becoming a victim of your own unrealistic status expectations, consider expanding your career options to include other work values such as time flexibility, low stress, challenge, and growth potential. Be increasingly open-minded to avoid financial drain. Look at all employment options, including working concurrent positions, temporary and contract positions, entrepreneurial ventures, and self-employment. Don't wait until you are financially desperate.

## Unrealistic Salary Expectations

As a mature worker, you should be proud of the salary level you have achieved. After all, you've worked hard for many years to develop your competencies. But you also need to recognize that the employment market has its own rule of supply and demand. The rule is that an excess of workers to fill open positions, coupled with negative economic conditions, drives salaries down.

As an older worker, you are often competing with younger workers who have the requisite job experience without the higher price tag. In other words, an employer may appreciate your 15 years of project management experience, but be willing to get by with 8 years for a lower cost. The hiring manager may have a number of candidates from which to select and be rewarded for keeping her business profitable.

I met Sabrina while speaking at the Crossroads Career Network, a free national nondenominational ministry. She was five months into her career search and becoming concerned about the financial drain of unemployment. As we talked, I discovered that she had failed to consider a number of offers because they were $10,000 to $15,000 less than she had been making. At that time, the field had a glut of unemployed project managers. My advice to her was this: "Entertain offers. You may be able to negotiate up or receive a sign-on bonus. Don't hold out any longer."

Fortunately, Sabrina accepted my advice. Although she took a 10 percent salary cut, her new employer is age diverse; she is challenged in her work; and her commute is significantly less. Plus, she can keep her resume up to date and continue networking. As the supply and demand for her position changes, she can resume her job search. Additionally, statistics show that until 2015, older workers will be in higher demand because of an increasing labor shortage due to a declining birthrate in the Gen-Xers.

## Career Tunnel Vision

Frequently the stress of unemployment or misemployment causes tunnel vision. You may fail to recognize the many opportunities available to you in the job market because you are grieving over lost opportunities or suffering from low self-esteem. What can you do if you are in this predicament? Sandy found herself in this situation.

Sandy was 63 years old when her husband died unexpectedly. She had taken an early retirement as an executive secretary at 55, counting on her husband to work until he was 65 and to invest their money wisely. Unfortunately, Sandy's husband had invested exclusively in technology, and as she became involved in their finances, she realized that she would need to return to work within a year.

When Sandy came to me, she was experiencing tunnel vision. She was still grieving over her husband, feeling angry about his investments, and suffering from the "poor me" syndrome. We had a lot of work to do. When you are suffering from disappointment, anger, fear, or other negative emotions, it can be hard to see any blessing in your situation. The first thing I did was to honor Sandy's emotions. She shared them with me so that we could move on.

Sandy needed to work, but she was no longer interested in being an executive secretary. I suggested that she take a career assessment, the Myers-Briggs Type Inventory, to explore her career options. I assured her that our partnership would help her design a new career that would be enjoyable and marketable in today's economic climate.

Sandy's career assessment indicated a strong interest in the medical field. After research, she settled on a career as an MRI technician, tapping into the growing need for these professionals in the healthcare industry. Sandy attended a month-long class, consisting of class work and clinical training. The cost was under $3,000. When she graduated, her expected income potential was $46,000 to $55,000. She is excited about her future prospects and is no longer suffering from tunnel vision.

## Reluctance to Apply for Unemployment Compensation

Many people are reluctant to or unaware that they can apply for unemployment compensation. If you are unemployed due to no fault of your own, in most cases, you are eligible for unemployment compensation for 26 weeks. In some cases, states are offering extended benefits during hard economic times.

Each state has its own rules. Most states have a two- to three-week waiting period, so if you have been downsized, apply as soon as possible through your local state unemployment office. A good source for general information about unemployment compensation is the U.S. Department of Labor's Employment and Training Administration Web site (www.doleta.gov).

My clients have shared that they have had positive experiences with state unemployment offices. There is no stigma attached to receiving unemployment benefits while you are unemployed. State offices are upbeat and provide training resources in job search skills, along with opportunities for retooling and training if your current position is no longer marketable. I encourage you to take advantage of these complimentary services.

## Managing the Emotional Roller-Coaster of Career Search and Career Management

Career transition is like riding a roller-coaster. You may feel elated one day because you have completed your *Wow!* ageless resume. The next day you may not want to get out of bed because you are tired of making your networking calls. By the end of the week you are thrilled; you have an interview set up for your ideal job.

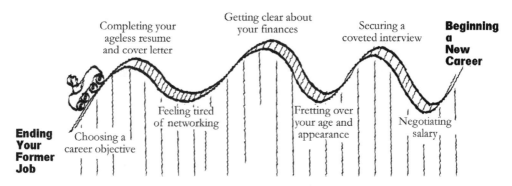

*The career roller-coaster.*

There is no getting around it or avoiding the ups and downs of career transition, but you can minimize your stress with the following positive steps:

- Recognize that your up-and-down mood swings are normal. Get professional help if your negative feelings last too long or are extreme.

- Allow yourself time off for fun, and engage in different activities that give you a fresh perspective.

- Write about your successes and concerns in a daily journal.

- Exercise and engage in your version of mindless meditation.

- Meet and communicate with friends and family and continue to develop your support systems.

- Spend time in nature.

- Develop a new hobby.

- Participate in volunteer activities.

When you have successfully landed or created your new job or jobs, take care of yourself. Keep your resume updated, your appearance fresh, your skills cutting edge, and your network growing! After all, you may want to work a lot longer than you ever imagined.

# INDEX